What's in Your Space?

For our families and staff, without whom this work would not have happened

What's in Your Space?

5 Steps for Better School and Classroom Design

Dwight Carter

Gary Sebach

Mark White

CORWIN
A SAGE Publishing Company

FOR INFORMATION:

Corwin

A SAGE Company

2455 Teller Road

Thousand Oaks, California 91320

(800) 233-9936

www.corwin.com

SAGE Publications Ltd.

1 Oliver's Yard

55 City Road

London EC1Y 1SP

United Kingdom

SAGE Publications India Pvt. Ltd.

B 1/I 1 Mohan Cooperative Industrial Area

Mathura Road, New Delhi 110 044

India

SAGE Publications Asia-Pacific Pte. Ltd.

3 Church Street

#10-04 Samsung Hub

Singapore 049483

Acquisitions Editor: Ariel Price

Editorial Assistant: Andrew Olson

Production Editor: Amy Schroller

Copy Editor: Mark Bast

Typesetter: C&M Digitals (P) Ltd.

Proofreader: Dennis Webb

Indexer: Scott Smiley

Cover Designer: Scott Van Atta

Marketing Manager: Anna Mesick

Printed in the United States of America

ISBN 978-1-5063-2307-7

This book is printed on acid-free paper.

Certified Chain of Custody
Promoting Sustainable Forestry
www.sfiprogram.org
SFI-01268

SFI label applies to text stock

16 17 18 19 20 10 9 8 7 6 5 4 3 2 1

Contents

Publisher's Acknowledgments

Corwin gratefully acknowledges the editorial insight and guidance of the following reviewers:

Sean Beggin, Associate Principal
Anoka-Hennepin Secondary
    Technical Education Program
Anoka, MN

Marisa Burvikovs, Teacher
LaGrange School District
LaGrange Park, IL

David Clark, Curriculum and
    Technology Specialist
Butler County ESC
Hamilton, OH

Susan Imamura
Principal (Retired)
Honolulu, Hawaii

Virginia Kelsen, Executive
    Director, Instruction
Chaffey Joint Union High
    School District
Ontario, CA

Neil MacNeill, Head Master
Ellenbrook Independent
    Primary School
Ellenbrook, Western Australia

Jadi Miller, Director of Curriculum
    and Professional Development
Lincoln Public Schools
Lincoln, NE

Brooke Menduni, Assistant
    Principal
Dublin City Schools
Dublin, OH

Tricia Pena, High School Principal,
    Retired; Education Consultant
E.C.H.O. 360 Education
    Consulting
Vail, AZ

Renee Peoples, Teaching and
    Learning Coach
West Elementary School
Bryson City, NC

Carol Francesca Spencer, Director
    of Curriculum
Addison Northwest Supervisory
    Union
Vergennes, VT

About the Authors

Dwight Carter is the highly respected principal of New Albany High School, a high school in New Albany, Ohio, that is regularly ranked among the top 100 high schools in the nation. Prior to accepting the position at New Albany High School, he was the principal of Gahanna Lincoln High School, in Gahanna, Ohio, and played a key role in the design of Clark Hall and the implementation of global skills and technology into its curriculum. In 2013 he was named a national Digital Principal of the Year by the National Association of Secondary School Principals (NASSP). He is also an inductee in the Josten Renaissance National Hall of Fame because of his incredible work in developing positive student culture. Mr. Carter has frequently been a guest speaker at schools and universities and at local, state, and national conferences that deal with Generation Z's technology usage, staff development, school culture, and other 21st century education topics. He has authored numerous blogs and has written on behalf of NASSP. During his 22-year career, he has also been a high school social studies teacher, a high school assistant principal, and a middle school principal.

Gary Sebach is a LEED accredited professional architect currently serving as the director of architecture at OHM Advisors, an architecture, engineering, and planning firm located in Ohio, Michigan, and Tennessee. Gary has led multidisciplinary teams through designing all types of facilities, yet his ability to create dynamic and progressive educational facilities and corporate campuses has defined his 30-year career. His experience includes working with Fortune 500 giants including Cardinal Health, IGS Energy, and BMW Financial Services, as well as working with school districts throughout Ohio. A firm advocate of 21st century education trends, Gary's designs foster creativity and collaboration while supporting the variety of learning and working styles of students. He recently presented "21st Century Education Through the Lens of an Architect" at the Michigan Association of School Boards (MASB) annual conference and was a featured speaker at the 2013 American

Planning Association Ohio Chapter presentation "From Pavement to Partnership: The Clark Hall Story."

 **Mark White** is a school leadership and training consultant. Previously, he was the director of education and outreach at Mindset Digital, and the AP academic principal of the International Department of the Beijing National Day School in Beijing, China. As the superintendent of the Gahanna-Jefferson Public Schools in Gahanna, Ohio, he played a key role in the design of Clark Hall and the implementation of global skills and technology into its curriculum. During his tenure as superintendent, the district earned the state's highest academic ranking, opened Clark Hall, and achieved financial stability. During his 32-year career, Mr. White has been a consultant to both the College Board and ACT and has served on two national education reform committees. He has frequently been a guest speaker at schools and universities and at local, state, and national conferences. Earlier in his career, Mr. White was an assistant superintendent, high school principal, assistant principal, high school English teacher and department head, and band director.

Introduction

Our journey into new types of learning space came about through necessity. We were two school administrators and an architect in search of a better building, and we were part of a team that brainstormed, researched, planned, and then finally built a new type of high school building designed around global skills, the learning styles of 21st century learners, and student use of technology. The building is Clark Hall, an award-winning addition that is a part of Gahanna Lincoln High School in Gahanna, Ohio.

But this book is not just about learning space; it's also about the process of reinvention. When dreaming up Clark Hall we questioned nearly everything we knew about teaching, learning, and designing a building for high school students. We kept what we thought was relevant for today's students, and we gently moved the rest of it to the side. Building Clark Hall was both the most exciting and frightening experience of our professional lives—exciting because we saw the vast potential in the concept, yet frightening because we were placing our efforts (and around 20 million taxpayer dollars) into a new type of building the likes of which had not been constructed.

Since the opening of Clark Hall, we have found other educators around America who have gone through a similar process in various sorts of learning spaces. Some have redesigned parts of existing schools or individual classrooms, and a few have gotten to build a new structure from the ground up. They, too, know that just changing the learning space without changing practices will provide minimal improvement. We have to change the space in our heads to use the space in our environment. Twenty-first century teaching is more than a room; it's a state of mind.

Though Clark Hall has been a success (and was honored nationally by Scholastic as being one of the Best in Tech 2012), we are also quick to tell people that Clark Hall is not perfect; like any other environment, it is what you make of it. This is not a book in which we claim to have all of the answers and to have created an educational Utopia. Yet enough educators and students have adjusted their practices in Clark Hall to show the concept works. We have also heard from other teachers elsewhere in America who are using similar tactics in new types of space and are also seeing success. Like them, we are not turning back. We know this is the way forward.

We salute the educators who have been brave enough to begin to ask questions about their teaching and classroom design and those who will read this book and decide that they, too, want to begin taking steps into a new way to use learning space. We hope this book inspires them and guides them. It is designed around the five most important steps that we took during our own transformation: (1) understanding today's students (Generation Z) and designing user-friendly spaces that can help them to learn; (2) the need to ask essential questions of what we are trying to accomplish today with teaching, learning, and the use of space; (3) the difficulty of shifting our thinking to a 21st century mindset; (4) the necessity of implementing global skills into our curriculum and how they can be augmented through different types of space; and (5) the importance of allowing students to have access to powerful technology that will help them to maximize their learning throughout the new learning space.

The professional development activities in this book are designed to provide points for discussion and concrete steps that can be used to transition into a 21st century learning space. Many of them are built around the global skills we want to see our students use today—collaboration, critical thinking, creativity, and communication. Just as importantly, there are questions at the end of most chapters in subsections titled "Stretch to the Future" that encourage educators to extend their thinking and questions into areas in which there might not yet be clear answers. If we as educators are going to continue to evolve, then we must continue to push our imaginations into the next stage of 21st century teaching and learning. We must prepare for the future now. But a word of warning: some of these discussions will not be easy—some of them will be difficult. Like student learning, our own learning at times is messy and emotional, and it takes a great deal of perseverance and work to find answers that are not always immediately recognizable.

Finally, whereas this book is K–12 in its scope, we know that it will probably be most beneficial to high school educators. Whereas most elementary and middle school teachers have traditionally recognized the importance of flexible learning space, we know some are pushing their classroom design into new frontiers. To teach Generation Z, teachers at all levels must question their practices.

We wish you luck as you move forward with your efforts.

Dwight Carter
Columbus, Ohio

Gary Sebach
Columbus, Ohio

Mark White
Beijing, China

The Parable of the Sage and the Two Spaces

A sage visited a school, and the teachers gathered around her and said,

"Tell us about space."

And the sage replied,

"You have two types of space,

and how you use the first space will determine how you use the second space."

"But we have to worry about test scores," one of the teachers said,

"because our evaluations are tied to how our students score on the tests,

and we keep having our budgets cut,

and there's not much time to train on new methods,

and teachers are being laid off all over the world,

and everyone keeps telling us we're doing a poor job of teaching!"

The sage replied,

"You have two types of space,

and how you use the first space will determine how you use the second space."

"But it's so hard to teach today," said another teacher.

"We have to prepare our students for the global economy, so we have to keep changing what we teach,

and these students today are different than the ones we had 20 years ago.

They are part of Generation Z, and they want to use technology every hour of every day,

and our classrooms should look different but we don't know how to redesign them!"

The sage replied,

"You have two types of space,

and how you use the first space will determine how you use the second space."

Then one brave teacher said,

"If we are to survive then we must shift our thinking.

We must accept the new realities and adjust our classrooms."

The sage smiled and said,

"What happens here,"

and she reached out and gently touched the brave teacher on the forehead,

"will affect what happens here,"

and she motioned to the classroom space around her.

STEP 1

Understand Generation Z

As the world becomes more connected, educators everywhere are scrambling to find ways to adapt their teaching to keep up with their rapidly evolving world.

Some researchers who study societal trends have labeled this generation of students—those born after 2000—*Generation Z*. We've heard of Baby Boomers, Generation X, and Generation Y. All of those generations had to adapt and embrace a digital world, but the difference in Generation Z is that it is the first generation to be born into the digital age (Rothman, n. d.). Although Generation Z might adapt to a 20th century model, it is an unnatural fit, and our teaching and classroom design should be adjusted. Generation Z has spent its entire life with cell phones, computers, touch screens, and games. They have grown up in an anytime/anywhere world where varied information and entertainment options are always available at their fingertips, and they want this freedom of choice in all parts of their lives, including their lifestyles and learning styles. Educators know their students need global skills and technology, and the more educators learn about today's students the more they realize they need a new type of learning space.

This is not just an American initiative. Educators around the world are using their thinking space to transform their learning space.

The Beijing National Day School (BNDS) is one of China's premier public high schools. Its students come from throughout Beijing and every province in China, and they regularly achieve some of the highest scores in the world on College Board Advanced Placement tests and other American college readiness exams. Each year over 200 universities from North America, Europe, and Australia visit the school's campus on the west side of Beijing to recruit its students, who they recognize as being some of the finest in the world.

The international teaching staff at BNDS comes from 14 different countries. One of the teachers, Alejandra Rivera, is a native of Honduras and teaches business and economics. Rivera often incorporates global skills and the student use of technology into her curriculum. Students are often moving around the room, working together, and using their computers to demonstrate what they have learned. At times her current classroom feels too small for her activities. Like many other teachers, she dreams of having a better space that will allow her—and her Generation Z students—to be more creative.

The more years I teach, the more I realize how inadequate our classrooms are for implementing creative and innovative lesson plans for today's students. Aligned desks work great for lectures; however, we need to teach them skills that prepare them for jobs of the 21st century. I have learned that when I plan kinesthetic lessons, I get great results; kids remember more of the content being taught and they are more engaged rather than just preparing for a test.

The problem with planning kinesthetic lessons is actually having the right space for one. Currently, my classrooms are filled with 25 desks, and I have very little space left for moving them around. Rows and rows of desks do not lend themselves to collaborative learning or team-building activities.

If I could have a say how my ideal classroom would look, it would be huge, one that would allow me to create different areas so that we could move around according to the planned activities. I like to have big classrooms. In the past, when I have been lucky enough to have one, I have enjoyed greatly doing stations; this allows students to move around, maintains them engaged, and to go through different material in a fun, short way. I would like to have two big smart boards, one on each end of the classroom; two or more flip chart easels; microphones available so students get used to talking into them; and several plants spread around the classroom.

On one corner of the room, I would have a big rug, just like the one we used to sit on when in kindergarten. One is never too old for storytelling, even if now the topics are about economics or business studies. For example, we recently read Chapter 1 of the book Freakonomics, and the rug space would have been useful to sit there and discuss the reading in a more relaxed space that would allow the students to feel more comfortable sharing their ideas or asking questions about the reading.

I would like to have beanbag chairs spread around the room so students can sit and read near big windows that could be opened, and there would be walls with colorful art or posters, creating an environment that would create a better setting for reading.

As for the tables, I would like to have round tables that would encourage collaborative learning and would be great for discussion and teamwork projects. We do several group projects, and having round tables allows the kids to share their ideas with each other and collaborate in problem-solving activities. In my business class, when starting the unit of leadership, we did the Marshmallow Challenge and then we did a reflection on the leadership style that emerged in each member during the activity. Having them work in round tables would have been better.

I believe we should also have long working tables in a part of the classroom with baskets filled with tons of markers, colors, Legos, and art and craft materials. Creativity flows when given a creative setting. They should be allowed to be crafty in any of the projects that are assigned to them. We recently played economic charades, and I thought a flip chart easel would have worked perfectly. Another example was when they had to create a poster of an economic system (traditional, command, and market), and they had to describe the economic system, show how they could answer the three basic economic questions, explain the pros and cons, and show an example, all this using only 20 words. At first the kids were stressed out, and they said it was impossible, but they were creative and were able to allocate the scarcity of words properly, which was another topic they had already learned in economics—scarcity. I believe it's fun to give kids challenges of creating things; this enhances their critical-thinking skills and teaches them how to work in teams.

In a separate room of the school, I would love to have a room with a stage, like the TEDTalk stage, so students can have an accessible but formal stage to work on their presentation skills. A room with a big screen placed above the speaker, monitor with slides and timer for the speaker, some decoration, good lighting, and a recording system so students are able to record and see themselves present and work on weaknesses. I would also like a rolling mirror wall so students can roll it in front of them and see themselves and work on their mannerisms. This would be great for my business class, where we work hard on their presentation skills. (A. Rivera, personal communication, April 11, 2015)

Stages and Legos? Storytelling rugs and beanbag chairs? Some educators might say it's impossible to create such a space in their high school. Others might not fully understand Rivera's perspective on teaching 21st century students.

But some schools are already creating these types of learning spaces built around the needs of Generation Z. We can call them Z *Spaces*, which are classrooms, hallways, conference rooms, presentation rooms, or any other space in a school designed to meet the learning needs of Generation Z. They will look different and function in a different manner. Teachers like Rivera are embracing these Z Spaces. We need more Alejandra Riveras in the world, and we need schools that can help her to implement her vision.

The Beijing National Day School is responding—it is currently undergoing an extensive renovation that will make its teaching environment among the world's finest. Its administration understands the world has changed, and its students' needs are changing. The administration is applying a universal rule of teaching: *know your students.*

That rule is especially pertinent today as our students have evolved from receivers of information to interactive participants in their learning. But as educators, we are often so busy keeping up with the changes in education and our government mandates that we have trouble keeping up with the societal changes occurring around us. As we redesign our learning space, it is imperative that we understand the students who will be using it.

Debra Jasper is the CEO of Mindset Digital, and she has a firm understanding of the challenge before us. Prior to forming her company, she was an award-winning investigative reporter and directed the Kiplinger Program in Public Affairs Journalism at The Ohio State University. She has studied the trends shaping our society, especially those related to social media, and today she travels the world helping Fortune 500 executives to shift their thinking to understand their clients who live in a digital world. She encourages educators to think differently, too.

In today's social world, it's easy to get a message out. Think Twitter, Instagram, Snapchat, Pinterest, Vine, Periscope—there are more channels than ever. What's hard is getting a message in, getting hyperdistracted students to tune in to what you have to say. To capture attention, teachers today have to stay up to speed on the latest technologies and approaches.

Savvy teachers and administrators know they can't just ignore all of this anymore. Students need to learn not only how to use new platforms but how to use them safely and effectively. Today's educators get that there are two ROIs. The first is the return on investment in teaching students how to use technologies. And the second is the risk of ignoring—educators can't just ignore social media platforms where one out of seven people on earth are spending their time.

Today's attention span is 8 seconds on average. Eight seconds. That doesn't mean students won't tune in longer. Clearly, many of them will play video games or text their friends for hours. The 8-second attention span simply means that all of us are making snap decisions about whether your content is worth our time.

That means teachers today must not only adopt new technologies and approaches but also understand that social media is changing everything else they do. Their classroom presentations need to contain more visuals and less text, for example (in our 1-hour keynote presentations, for example, we typically show more than 350 highly visual slides). And teachers' notes to students and parents must be shorter and more skimmable. All of their communications—whether they are communicating to students, parents, administrators, or even their own colleagues—must be clear, to the point, and relevant.

You first need to help students adopt a new mindset before they will want to learn a new skill set. So schools across the country need to understand that social media has dramatically changed student expectations. They are looking to learn in environments that are more informal, engaging, and real-time. After all, there are no education rules that say you have to be boring.

At the same time, we emphasize that casual does not mean careless. It simply means more personable, entertaining, and fun.

Teachers who learn how to shift away from creating old-school, "blackboard" type content and into producing lively, informative classroom presentations that take advantage of Twitter, Vine videos, Periscope, and other technologies will better understand how to both inform and entertain. And today, if you want students to tune in, you must engage them first. There are no captive audiences, even in the classroom. (D. Jasper, personal communication, May 24, 2015)

As Jasper points out, today's generation of young people has different expectations.

Those of us teaching this generation had to immigrate into the digital world, but today's students are natives who have been shaped by it. So, shouldn't we shape our learning space around Generation Z? As we shift our thinking in what we teach and how we teach to create these Z Spaces, let's consider the characteristics and needs of the young people of Generation Z.

THE IMPORTANCE OF CELL PHONES

First, Generation Z students tend to be connected to their peers 24/7, and they panic when they don't have access to their devices. A cell phone is more than a tool for making phone calls: it is a storage area for texts and a vital repository for the phone numbers that form a students' social hub. In their minds, to lose a phone or to lose connectivity is to be cast adrift socially. Our high schools are filled with stories of normally mild-mannered students who have acted irrationally when their cell phones are confiscated, stolen, or lost. They've always had access to a cell phone, and to carry one is as natural as Baby Boomers carrying wallets. They are not necessarily addicted to their devices but addicted to the connection. Unlike their predecessors, many students today do not wear wristwatches. When they need to check the time, they look at their cell phones. They are the most important objects they carry each day, more important than any textbook or binder.

CONNECTED THROUGH SOCIAL MEDIA

Generation Z students are connected. Our students interact with a multitude of online sites, and this is the mode they often use to communicate and to think. They might call each other on the phone, but they will often tweet or use some other form of social media to quickly send their thoughts to a friend—often in fewer than 140 characters.

THE INFLUENCE OF GAMING

Gaming has shaped their brains and learning. Generation Z students are used to solving problems, sometimes alone and sometimes online with others. The parts of their brains that process images have become more developed than those of previous generations, which means they respond positively to imagery, bright colors, and movement. When presented with a visual problem, they want to figure it out as they would a video game. In a video game they are given constant feedback, and when they conquer a step they are rewarded by moving on to the next level. Some of them have grown up being connected to other young people from around the world through online gaming, either as teammates in pursuit of the same gaming goals or as competitors. This has forced them to be digital problem solvers.

WORKING IN SMALL GROUPS

Because of their constant connectivity, Generation Z students are used to interacting with small groups (Rothman), and this connectivity makes it easier for them to find times and places to meet in person, such as the local Starbucks, where they can sit, talk, study, game, check messages, tweet, text, and watch streaming videos and TV shows all at the same time. As we redesign our space, let's allow them to have areas to work in small groups, to spread out, and choose seating in an environment that fits their personality and task. These students can carry pens, pencils, and binders, but writing by hand on paper is less natural than typing. They will need spaces where they can sit comfortably and use a tablet or laptop. This space can be in a classroom, in a small conference room, or in a hallway. If we walk down any hallway in many schools today, we will see students sitting outside of classrooms in student desks they've carried into the hallway or they will be sitting on the floor. The hallways have often been turned into impromptu learning spaces; it's time they were actively designed to be learning spaces. A few pieces of furniture placed in key hallways can provide viable options to support small-group learning.

IT'S ALL ABOUT THE INTERNET

When Generation Z students want to figure something out, they turn to Google, YouTube, Vine, or the Comedy Channel. They're not going to go to the media center to find a book. Instead they'd rather watch a video, and they want the information delivered quickly and in small meaningful chunks. They will spend an average of 8 seconds scanning a page for links or fast-forwarding through a video (Rothman). The students of Generation Z don't believe in e-mail; they'd rather text, tweet, Snapchat, or message someone. E-mails are too long and take too much time to compose and read.

MEMORIZATION AND MOTIVATION

Students today can memorize information for our tests, but they know they will be using their cell phones and tablets to Google information when they are outside of school. Memorization is only done in school to achieve a grade, which calls into question the role of memorization in a 21st century classroom. All students need to have a core set of factual understandings on which to build and apply knowledge, but where is the line between building that set and asking students to memorize information they could just as easily Google?

The deepest learning often occurs when the content is meaningful and not just when the content is memorized to achieve an external reward. Ideally, we could work with our students to have them prove to us in some other creative manner that they have mastered concepts. Consequently, this calls into question the use of grades in 21st century classrooms. We must ask if it is more effective to have students work to achieve grades or to achieve knowledge—sometimes they coincide and sometimes they do not.

And if we can build a system where students are motivated by the curriculum and the type of assessment they are using, will they want to be in class more and be there on time? At the secondary level, what should be the role of bells in calling students to class and dismissing them? Are they still needed? Can students make it to class on time because they wish to learn and are not responding to a bell? This is a discussion for each staff and one that can be had with students. There are no easy answers.

THE IMPORTANCE OF RELATIONSHIPS

As we reexamine our philosophy, practices, and learning space to teach Generation Z, we must also remember that it has commonalities with other generations we have taught. These students still need friends and a sense of belonging. Though they might be connected to a wide circle through social media, we must give them opportunities to interface and form personal bonds with their peers and teachers. Regardless of their online learning activities or their ability to function online independently, they still need access to high-quality, motivated, professional educators who care about them and their progress. It's possible the freedoms to which they must be exposed in their learning will necessitate more guidance than ever from educators. They are used to multitasking, but this doesn't necessarily mean they can complete complicated tasks when doing so, and Generation Z has more questions about its future jobs than any other generation, because so many of those jobs do not exist yet. Our students need us more than ever.

BEGIN TAKING STEPS—NOW!

Another educator who sees the potential of the Z Space being created at the Beijing National Day School is Santosh Madhavan. He has successfully taught physics to young people for over 30 years and knows he must continue to evolve with his students. For example, in his classroom today he has his students download apps onto their cell phones to use in labs. However, when his students complete the labs they often bump into each other and struggle to be heard over the conversations of their peers and the noise of the apps. He knows his kinesthetic teaching could be more effective if he had a variety of spaces to use.

Madhavan asks some fair questions about why our schools look alike and if we really need to keep building the same types of space.

> Educational institutions are slow to react to changes. The inertia of the system has a whole host of reasons but is often the inability for the decision makers to foresee changes. Educators involved with designing schools should get ahead of the curve by adopting a new perspective in assigning space for classroom use. Fundamentally, it is sound to ask oneself, do we keep doing the same thing over and over again? In the future, are students going to sit at desks to hear teachers lecture? At the very least, should we not be thinking about how education will evolve in the light of freely available powerful handheld and wearable digital devices and how that would affect the use of space in schools? (Madhavan, personal interview, May 1, 2015)

To repeat what Madhavan asks, do we keep doing the same thing over and over again?

As the Chinese philosopher Lao Tzu said, "A journey of a thousand miles begins with a single step." It's time to begin taking steps to create space for our Generation Z students.

PROFESSIONAL DEVELOPMENT
IDEAS TO UNDERSTAND GENERATION Z
Collaborate

- Discuss the school's cell phone policy and determine if it is adequate for working with Generation Z.

- Ask your students which social media sites they use and how they use them.

- Poll your students about their online gaming habits and ask about the most difficult problem they have solved in one stage of their favorite game.

- Ask your students which site they go to online when they need a fast answer to a question.

- Ask your fellow educators and your students how much material should be memorized today and how that material should be chosen.

- Ask your students what motivates them outside of school. Discuss the positive and negative effect of grades with your students.

- Turn the bells off for one day and discuss the results with your colleagues and students.

- Start discussing with students the concept of using different kinds of furniture in classrooms. Begin to open up their minds to being partners in helping you to choose chairs, desks, and other types of furniture of the new learning space.

Think Critically

- Read books, look at websites, or watch videos about the characteristics of Generation Z.

Here are some recommended books.

- o *Teaching the Digital Generation: No More Cookie-Cutter High Schools*, Frank Kelly, Ted McCain, and Ian Jukes
- o *A Whole New Mind*, Daniel Pink
- o *Digital Leadership: Changing Paradigm for Changing Times*, Eric Sheninger
- o *Creative Confidence*, Chip and Dan Heath
- o Corwin Connected Educators series

- Watch these videos and discuss their major points.
  - Sir Ken Robinson, *Do Schools Kill Creativity?* TEDTalk
  - Sir Ken Robinson, *Bring on the Learning Revolution* TEDTalk
  - Salman Khan, *Let's Use Video to Reinvent Education* TEDTalk
  - Ramsey Mussallam, *3 Rules to Spark Learning* TEDTalk

Create

- Ask your students to help you create ways to use social media in the school to share information or give assignments.
- Create social media guidelines for students and staff.

Communicate

- Use social media to share the results of your discussions about Generation Z with your community.

Stretch to the Future

- Meet periodically and discuss trends being exhibited by students. Continue to research it to see what others are thinking.

Research

Study three sources of research (e.g., books, articles, blogs, videos) about Generation Z. List what each source says about Generation Z and discuss the commonalities.

SOURCE 1 TITLE:	SOURCE 2 TITLE:	SOURCE 3 TITLE:
What does this source say about Generation Z?	What does this source say about Generation Z?	What does this source say about Generation Z?

Analysis of Current Practices

Analyze your current practices and determine which ones are conducive to teaching Generation Z and which ones need to be adjusted as you prepare to design a new type of learning space. Some of the practices are listed for you. Feel free to add to the list.

PRACTICES THAT FIT THE LEARNING STYLES THAT WILL BENEFIT GENERATION Z	IS THIS PRACTICE ALREADY OCCURRING IN YOUR CLASSROOM?	WHAT CAN YOU DO TO ADJUST THE PRACTICE?	DO YOU HAVE OTHER IDEAS OR SUGGESTIONS?
Cell phone policy			
Use of social media			
Group work			
Online research			
24/7 learning			

PRACTICES THAT FIT THE LEARNING STYLES THAT WILL BENEFIT GENERATION Z	IS THIS PRACTICE ALREADY OCCURRING IN YOUR CLASSROOM?	WHAT CAN YOU DO TO ADJUST THE PRACTICE?	DO YOU HAVE OTHER IDEAS OR SUGGESTIONS?
Student choice in working space			
Student options in the curriculum and assessment			
Bell schedule			
Blended learning opportunities			

Transitioning to the New Space

The move into the new space is more than a physical move; it is also a mental move for all parties. Begin to make the transition to the new space before the space is actually used.

Start asking your students what features they want in the new learning space. Ask them about paint colors, furniture preferences, natural lighting, and what can be done with the space to make it both efficient and fun.

If an architect is involved in the space redesign, what discussions have you had with the architect to share ideas about Generation Z?

Begin a dialogue with students about how they will be able to use the new space efficiently, ethically, and in a mature manner.

Other ideas:

STEP 2

Start Asking Questions

When we created Clark Hall, an award-winning Z Space in Gahanna, Ohio, we started with lots of questions that ended in a new type of building. It's not like we had a sudden vision of the process from the first to the last step. The answers came one by one. At times we felt like three carpenters who had built houses for years—and suddenly realized we needed to build a new type of skyscraper. There were days when we nailed a philosophical plank into place and asked each other, "What do you think?" We would look at each other, check our sources, talk about it, adjust it, and then begin to hammer the next plank.

We tell you this so you will know that whereas redesigning learning space is exciting and challenging, there is no one way to do it. Every trek into space redesign will be unique.

The new spaces will have commonalities, but they will all look different and have original characteristics. To redesign a learning space is to mirror what we do each day in our classrooms: we step into the unknown, delve into the inner space of others, and attempt to build something beautiful and lasting.

But to fully understand our journey into a new type of learning space, we have to go back in time—all the way back to the last century.

And we have to start asking questions.

OUR BEGINNING

The three of us were products of 20th century thinking. We all went to good schools and had successful careers. Two of us were educators and the other was an architect who helped design hundreds of schools. We knew school space because we had spent time in so many schools. We thrived within the traditional system.

But then the global economy emerged, education started to reform, and we began to notice our students weren't quite the same as the ones we had known before. These new students lived with cell phones and computers, and they wanted choices 24 hours per day. They hung out in coffee shops and talked via social media.

The system we knew so well was changing.

We wondered if we needed to change, too. We began to discuss it with some of our fellow educators. Some of them said, "We need to change, but we don't know how."

Others told us they didn't need to change. They said, "We have to teach these kids in straight rows and do what we've always done because when they get to college this is how it will be."

We starting asking more difficult questions like, "Are there some fundamental new points we need to adopt to teach today's students? Isn't the best way to run a classroom to design instruction around student learning, not just in ways we already knew how to teach? If we really improved learning, wouldn't Generation Z students be able to use their skills to adapt to any future system, regardless of their college or their profession?" These questions began to shake our philosophical foundations.

We were beginning to adjust our inner space.

OUR SHIFT

Then something happened that ultimately changed our view of teaching forever: we had to build a new building. Our high school that was designed for 2,000 students was being used by over 2,300 young people. We needed more learning space, not an entire school but an addition.

At first we discussed adding a new block of classrooms that would match what we already had in our current school. But then we asked, "If we apply our new practices in this building, does this learning space have to be like all of the other traditional schools, the kind we've always built?" It seems in the past whenever we've needed more space we've just added a new wing that functions like all the others without really asking if this was the best way to design learning space. We just went back to what we knew and were comfortable with. We even went to great pains to make sure it looked like the old school.

The world had changed, and our students had changed. We knew we had to change. We knew we needed a new type of learning space.

Here are two important tips about the scale of your space redesign:

1. You don't have to start from the ground up to create a new type of learning space. Whereas we were fortunate enough to build an entire new building, many schools and individual teachers might just change their learning space one space at a time. Schools and teachers can start with a corner of a classroom or an entire classroom, a hallway, or just one part of an

existing space. It doesn't matter if the building is relatively new or several decades old.

2. Your space redesign doesn't have to cost millions of dollars—or even hundreds of dollars. If all you can do is begin with a small project and a small budget (and perhaps with donated goods and services) then that's at least better than not changing any of your space. Budgets everywhere in education are tight; more than ever before educators need to be creative in finding resources. Remember the old saying: where there's a will there's a way! (Tips for finding resources are given in Step 3.)

LISTENING TO OTHERS

We kept talking to the people around us. At first we heard, *You gotta have lockers . . . and you gotta have bells . . . and you gotta go out and buy some of those student desks where students can slide their text books under their seats during class . . . and you can't have too many windows these days because of security . . . and you gotta put your school colors everywhere to remind students to have school spirit . . . but most of the walls have to be white, because that's the easiest paint to use and all the walls need to look the same . . . and all of the rooms need to be the exact same size . . . the halls are just for getting from one place to another . . .*

But we wondered if modern high schools still needed these things, so we talked with our most important experts—our students. They said, *Most of us have backpacks so we don't use lockers anymore . . . we don't always need bells . . . we want comfortable furniture . . . we love big windows and natural light . . . school colors don't give us school spirit, spirit comes from feeling good about the school . . . we want bright colors . . . we don't care about the room size . . . we sit in the halls sometimes to work so it would be nice to have some comfortable furniture out there . . .*

We talked to teachers, administrators, and parents. They told us, *We like new things, but we feel safe with the old things. Will new ideas work? Will students like them? Will a new type of learning space help our kids get into college?*

We started pulling ideas together and sharing our thoughts. We found adjusting to change and to new methods is a difficult concept for some people to accept. Throughout history, individuals who have come up with new ideas have often heard negative statements that are meant to stop them, including anyone who has tried radical new concepts in schools. Here are some of the comments we heard.

It might lower my test scores.

That will never work here.

Our students could never do that.

We don't have the money.

But that's never been done before.

We tried something like that once, and it didn't work.

I don't have time.

This is crazy.

I don't know how.

This might affect my evaluation.

These sorts of comments have been heard in schools for many years, and we call them dream killers—because they are spoken to try to kill the dreams

▶ Gahanna-Jefferson Public Schools

of those who seek better ways of teaching and learning. They are often spoken out of fear by people who might lack the vision or capacity to evolve with the times. Schools should be vibrant places where dreams thrive, not museums where they are buried beneath the antiquated thinking of the previous century. Classrooms must not be factories where students produce grades; they must be studios where students create and their minds are set free.

CLEAR TALKING POINTS

After listening, talking, and doing our research, we formed three clear goals for the learning space in the building:

1. Global skills had to be the foundation of its curriculum (and throughout the rest of the district). The classrooms, hallways, and common spaces had to let students gather, collaborate, communicate, create, and foster critical thinking. We wanted the space to facilitate the learning.

2. The building had to fit the needs of Generation Z. It had to have bright colors, different kinds of furniture, lots of sunlight, and room for students to move around. A key part of 21st century learning is choice in how and where assignments are

completed, and this building had to allow for movement and flexibility.

3. Our students had to be able to use technology to complete most of their assignments, which means the technology infrastructure had to be so strong that it would be fast, reliable, and have the ability to expand as more and more devices came online.

We realized the three of us couldn't do it alone. When you are changing your part of the world, you need to bring the people who live there along with you, so we included a lot of different people in our plans and dreams.

And of course, we asked our students to join us.

A New Design Process for a New Type of Building

Students are often the untapped resource of education reform. We asked, "How many ways can we involve them?" We wanted the building to be shaped by their ideas.

Our students named the building. They researched the history of the building's location, and they suggested we name the building after a farmer who had owned the land in the 1800s. His last name was Clark, so the building became known as Clark Hall. In doing so, we tied the history of our community into the present. His land became a place where 21st century dreams are born.

Our students even researched colors and made recommendations for what color the interior walls should be. Some of them wanted bright colors in some areas and soothing colors in others, but almost all of them told us they were tired of white walls in classrooms. We purposely chose colors that would not match or coordinate in traditional color schemes. A bright green chair might be sitting on a vibrant orange carpet square.

▶ Gahanna-Jefferson Public Schools

Or a golden yellow ottoman might be placed on a red strip of carpet. In some rooms, the furniture might not match the colors of the walls; the walls might even clash with it. We didn't want to worry about matching colors when moving furniture around the building. We chose colors the students liked that were positive and vibrant.

We asked, "Can this building be a metaphor for how we view learning? Let's make it irregular, unpredictable, exciting, and fun."

▶ Gahanna-Jefferson Public Schools

Chairs Are for Thinking, Not Just Sitting

Then we took our students on field trips to furniture companies, especially ones that specialized in contemporary office furniture. We wanted chairs that were comfortable, bright, could be moved around, and could allow a student to relax or to use a laptop or read a book.

▶ Gahanna-Jefferson Public Schools

The furniture chosen included regular chairs, padded chairs, rocking chairs (purchased from the front porch of the local Cracker Barrel restaurant), and high-top tables and matching chairs. A few Adirondack chairs were added so that students and teachers could sit in the classroom and let their mind think they were at the beach. Other popular choices for sitting were exercise balls and ottomans on wheels that could be rolled around the room as students moved from group to group. We wanted the classrooms to be fun—we wanted students to have the freedom to choose the type of seating that worked best for them.

Desks Can Be Tools for Collaboration

Then we asked our students about their desks. Who needs square or rectangular desks anymore? Desks come in all kinds of shapes from squares to rectangles to triangles. We wanted to have desks that could allow students to work independently and just as importantly work in small groups because that's a hugely important global skill we were stressing in our classes. We learned that some desks were designed so that they could be placed beside other desks to form groups or circles. We chose desks that were shaped like isosceles trapezoids.

▶ Gahanna-Jefferson Public Schools

Carpet Diem

Who says you have to learn standing up or sitting up? Can you lie down and learn? Yes.

Many of the classrooms had carpet squares on the floors on which students could sit or lie down to read, type, surf the Internet, or talk. The students chose the colors of the squares. Upon entering Clark Hall, it would be typical to see students on the floor. It was one of the final traditional barriers to be broken. We thought of it as "carpet diem."

Creativity Is Contagious

We noticed something interesting when we spoke to vendors: everyone, even noneducators, got excited about changing schools and helping kids. The furniture representatives at the companies told us what would be durable and affordable—and they were excited about helping us. They told us they wished they'd had furniture like that when they were in high school. They would laugh and offer ideas, and the more we talked with them the more excited they became. When we spoke with the representatives from the technology firms, we could see they understood our vision and they enthusiastically offered advice and said they wanted to tour the building when it opened. Parents and community members would become enthused and offer to help. They all tapped into our dream. It was a reminder to us of the wonderful jobs we have. Each day we get to do what so many noneducators only dream of doing: we get to go into schools and work with young people. We get to help them grow.

▶ Gahanna-Jefferson Public Schools

▶ Gahanna-Jefferson Public Schools

Different Skills, Different Spaces

What types of buildings have long straight hallways with rooms on both sides that are the exact same size and look the same? Hotels, prisons, and schools.

We didn't want to design a hotel where students quickly come and go. Nor could we create a prison-like building where students would be asked to conform and to place their imagination on hold until they exited through the front doors.

In designing the classrooms, we purposely made them various sizes for different sorts of skill-based activities. Some were average sized, and some were larger than most traditional classrooms. The large rooms allowed for more space to spread out when the students were working on projects, and the intent was not to assign rooms on a permanent basis but to have teachers move around depending on what they were doing in class and how much space they needed.

There were small conference rooms between the classrooms that were filled with fun, functional furniture that could be used by small classes or by students who wanted quiet spaces or to work in small groups. The walls were painted various shades of yellow, orange, and green to brighten them up. Some rooms were in the interior of the building and others had exterior windows—which made them more popular with our students.

▶ Gahanna-Jefferson Public Schools

The future will be one of adaptability, and we wanted that trait in the building. The classrooms were located on two separate floors, and each floor had a large common space the size of three classrooms with movable walls that could subdivide the room when needed. The space could be used for students to work individually or to collaborate in groups, to host guest speakers, to be used for professional development of staff, or to be rented to community members for evening activities.

▶ Gahanna-Jefferson Public Schools

Hallways have always been extensions of classrooms, especially in high schools, so we said, "Let's make the hallways viable learning spaces." We put

▶ Gahanna-Jefferson Public Schools

various types of furniture in them to create spots for students to work quietly. In most classes, students could choose to work online in the classrooms with their teachers present, or they could work independently or in small groups in the conference rooms, halls, or in the common spaces.

▶ Gahanna-Jefferson Public Schools

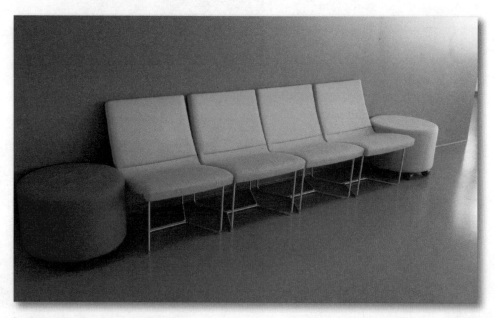

▶ Gahanna-Jefferson Public Schools

We also added a wall of clipboards, where students could write or draw whatever they wanted. We thought of it as a sort of a whimsical wall where they could have fun and be creative.

▶ Gahanna-Jefferson Public Schools

Most schools today are designed with small windows for security reasons. They're meant to keep the world out, but they also block out the sun. We took security seriously. Like other schools, we had police officers on campus and we monitored the entrances. But we chose to have huge windows that let in lots of natural light into the various spaces. We chose to dwell on the positive. We chose the sun as our silent partner.

▶ Gahanna-Jefferson Public Schools

▶ Gahanna-Jefferson Public Schools

The Importance of Technology

To implement the technology, we formed strategic partnerships with three of the great high-tech companies of the world: Dell, Intel, and Cisco. The representatives were so excited about the project that they made it afford-able for us, and we were able to buy new, powerful computers throughout the entire district and to upgrade the speed and capability of our technology for all buildings.

This allowed the technology to become the foundation of learning. A lot of people don't understand that the technology infrastructure, which forms the network, is often the key to technology success. If we have a weak infrastructure, new computers won't function as quickly or as consistently. It will take forever to log on, and the system will continue to crash. Putting new computers on an old network is like putting a Ferrari sports car on a small two-lane road: it can't go fast and is constantly stuck in traffic. And the more Ferraris you place on the road the worse it gets. Instead, we should think of the network as a wide Autobahn with lots of lanes where Ferraris can cruise at high speeds. A huge problem is that it's cheaper to buy computers than it is to expand the network, just like it's cheaper to buy a car than it is to implement a huge road improvement project. Districts often buy the computers but don't pay enough attention to the network or its maintenance.

As we planned the new building, we took steps to dramatically enhance our technology infrastructure. It was of high priority for us. We made sure we had a team that was large enough and talented enough to keep it all running. We even hired our own internal engineer to ensure we had continuity in our problem solving. It was a monumental task for the technology team, but when the building and the rest of the district finally got up and running, it was as strong of a program as any found in any district in the world.

Fostering Student Buy-In

Though our students had been assisting us in the building's design, we encountered a challenge during the building's construction that totally surprised us: some students told us they might be reluctant to use it in the following year when it opened. Their current building was all they had known, and they loved it and didn't want to leave it. The new building was across the street from the high school, and they feared they would lose their friends and connections to the school if they attended a few classes each day in the new building. To help our students make the transition, we arranged for some of them to take guided tours of the building in the final months before the building opened. When they walked through the building, looked out the windows and saw the old building nearby, and heard that some of their teachers would be teaching in the building, then they were relieved. When they saw how some of the spaces were being formed, they became excited. They went back and told their friends, who spread the word that the building was going to be a positive change.

A New Type of Building, a New Funding Formula . . . and New Challenges

Our questioning of traditional formats even extended into our funding for the building. We asked, "Do we have to fund this building in the same way we've always done it? Are we missing an opportunity to be creative and to explore a new path, especially in this era of shrinking budgets?"

Luckily, we found a different path.

We realized the location for Clark Hall was at one of the busiest intersections in the city. Thousands of people drove past it each day, which made it prime real estate. We were able to design Clark Hall with three stories and make it a mixed-use facility, which means the first floor would be leased to private companies and the second and third floors would be used by our juniors and seniors. The entire building was constructed in such a way that it can be easily converted to office space in the future if the district ever wishes to do so. The income from leasing the first floor, along with some other land on the site leased to a developer, would provide income to pay for the construction of the building.

Though the concept made the project affordable, it was a new idea for the community, and it took a lot of explaining and patience to help our citizens understand it. And, to make it even more challenging, the construction of Clark Hall began during the recent global recession. Some naysayers told us the mixed-use concept would never work. But we believed in the vision. When the building opened and the rest of the land was developed, it was quickly filled to capacity with tenants. The financial plan was successful, and the building's educational programming was extremely effective.

Experiencing tough times is not an excuse to quit.

Here is a tip for weathering a financial storm while developing a new learning space:

Clark Hall was built during the toughest recession to hit the American economy since the Great Depression, and the district was going through some horrendous budget cuts. It was difficult, but we remained focused on the mission of developing the space. The greatest organizations make tough choices, prioritize their funding to keep moving forward, and then they are poised for a rapid climb as they emerge from the financial crisis.

If the funding is difficult to find for your space redesign, then keep searching for new ways to do it, remain committed to the goal, and know that it can be done step by step over time. It might not be easy, but it's essential for students. Great educators have a passion that can't be stopped. Keep trying until you reach your goal.

▶ Gahanna-Jefferson Public Schools

The Importance of Selecting and Training Staff

Another challenge involved selecting and training the teachers who would be working in the new building. Not all of the teachers on the 150-member staff would be teaching in the building. Only 40 or so would be working there. A private, informal discussion was had with teachers who wanted to participate, and they were asked how they would use global skills in their curriculum, how they would allow students to use technology, and how they would incorporate the building's Generation Z features into their teaching and assessment. It's important to note that a great deal of professional development had taken place for many years with the staff to shift their thinking out of 20th century modes into a more global perspective. Internationally known speakers such as David Langford, Ian Jukes, and Tom Guskey had visited the district and spoken with our staff. We also had extensive training in Understanding by Design strategies and student benchmarking.

To deepen the discussion, when the teachers to work in the new building were selected they met weekly after school for discussions and planning. They cared so much they volunteered their time; we had a shared vision. Here is one of the documents created to summarize the vision for teaching and learning in the new building.

GJPS Lesson Plan Template for Student Learning

Part I: Desired Results of Student Learning

Goal(s):

Understanding(s):

Essential Question(s):

Graduate Profile Skills Covered:

Part II: Relevance to the Student

How will the student participate in the lesson design, instruction, and/or assessment?

Part III: Technology Used by the Student

What technology will the student use?

Part IV: Assessment of Student Progress

How will you and the student assess progress to ensure the student understands and can apply the material?

Part V: Action Plan for Student Learning

How will you and the student determine the key actions, the sequence, and the time frame for student learning?

Part VI: Rigor

How will you and the student define the rigor and the quality of the process and the evidence of learning?

Understanding That Educators Evolve at Different Speeds

When the building opened and the teachers began their work there, some moved quickly into new ways of teaching while others moved more slowly. Adults are like students: they are going to progress at different speeds based on their personalities, background, and the support they have. Throughout our careers, we have observed educators who have been vehemently opposed to change for various reasons; however, as they have become part of the change process they have shifted their perspective and become change advocates. We saw this same process in the new building with one teacher who was assigned to the building for schedule reasons and not for his teaching perspective. However, once he was in the building and began to observe other teachers, he transformed his own teaching.

SOMETIMES PEOPLE NEED TO SEE NEW IDEAS TO UNDERSTAND THEM

The construction of Clark Hall finished a few days before the start of school, and one evening we had a community-wide open house for people to tour it. We were overwhelmed by the interest shown and by the positive comments. A number of students, staff, and parents excitedly said, "Now that I see it I understand what you were talking about," and "I can see my child being successful in this building." Sometimes people have to see it, touch it, and experience it to understand it.

REMAINING TRUE TO OUR CORE VALUES

Moving toward the future didn't mean we had to discard all of our history. Throughout the entire process, we kept asking, "Who are we? Why are we doing this?"

We had a long tradition in our district of academic excellence balanced with a well-rounded education in the arts and extracurricular activities. Great organizations remain true to their core values—especially when they are reinventing their practices.

To keep our philosophy alive, we decided early in the process to be true to our three broad cornerstones as we designed our new space: (1) to provide an education that consisted of strong academics, (2) to keep our commitment to the arts and extracurricular activities, and (3) to recognize the need to be physically fit and to make healthy choices.

As we drew up the plans for the building, we knew the core academics would thrive there, but we intentionally included an art room. Although the new building was just one extension of the high school and we wouldn't have every type of class in it, it was a key decision to include art classes in the building because we wanted our students to see the importance of art in their lives. It's where they create and use critical thinking. It's one of the most important classes in a school. Plus, we wanted student art everywhere in the building. It was a building designed to maximize creativity—we wanted our students surrounded by art.

Like other communities around the country, we had concerns about the physical fitness of our students and staff. We know that creativity and critical thinking are often strengthened through physical activity. So we explored ways of moving fitness activities into the space. Eventually, we partnered with the local YMCA to give them a room in which they installed state-of-the-art exercise equipment. The room was open to our PE classes during the

school day, and time was allotted after school for staff members to work out. The room was granted to the YMCA in the evenings for public use. We also recognized the importance of extra-curricular sports in the district for their place in promoting fitness, collaboration, communication, and leadership.

When people walk into the building, the first things they see are three large banners that list these three cornerstones: Academics, The Arts, Athletics. On the opposite wall is a large image of our school mascot, a lion, that serves as a reminder to the students that they are part of a school and community.

AN EXAMPLE OF TEACHING IN A Z SPACE LIKE CLARK HALL

So how does a teacher effectively focus on teaching global skills, technology usage, and Generation Z in a new type of learning space? Exactly what does this look like in practice?

Prior to becoming an education consultant in Washington, D.C., Emily Sturchio was a high school English teacher who taught in Clark Hall. When asked to describe a typical day in her classroom and some of the projects undertaken by her students, Sturchio's reply demonstrates that she had accepted a 21st century teaching mindset in *what* students learned and *how* they learned in her classroom—and how she used her learning space.

On the first day of school in Clark Hall, the students entered my classroom with amazement. Rather than gazing upon uniform rows of desks and institutional beige walls decorated with dated motivational posters, they walked into a bright, colorful, and inviting space with couches, individual laptops, conference tables, exercise balls, a rocking chair, and more. One junior commented that it looked like Starbucks and immediately found his high-top table seat that looked out on the street.

But Clark Hall was more than a pretty face. This new environment provided me the space and flexibility I had desired throughout my decade-long teaching career, allowing me to incorporate the instructional methods, technology, and best practices that engage Gen Z students and promote critical thinking, creativity, collaboration, and communication. As a result, my time at Clark Hall brought about the most engaged—and perhaps the most successful—students I have ever had.

A TYPICAL DAY

To get the most out of this 21st century learning space required three major shifts in how I approached my teaching. The first shift was how I structured my class. No longer bound by the 45-minute race to fit in everything, I now had 90 minutes of time and lots of space to utilize. A typical class period looked something like this:

- Students came in, grabbed their computers, moved to their space both in and out of the classroom, and read independently.

- Students returned to class at the appointed time and I directed students to our class website. We reviewed the day's agenda and discussed upcoming deadlines and other details.

- I introduced new material and taught lessons, delivering all materials and assignments electronically through our classroom website.

- Students had open time (about 45 minutes to an hour) to work on various activities and assignments for the class. Students chose the best environment within the school to support their learning.

- I walked around the school and checked in with students to answer questions, teach mini-lessons, and provide assistance.

- Students returned to the classroom, and we wrapped up the lesson.

Giving students so much open time can be a little scary. It's important to accept that students may not always use their time in a way that you

(Continued)

(Continued)

think they should. In a traditional classroom, I had control of their time and managed every minute of it. In Clark Hall, I set deadlines and procedures, but students had choice in how and when they completed their work. I remember worrying about a student who was working on science during class and not his upcoming *Death of a Salesman* essay. I pulled him aside and inquired about his progress, thinking he would give me a litany of excuses for why he hadn't done his work. Instead, he pulled up a draft on his laptop complete with tracked changes, which was more work than the rest of the class had done. I asked him when he wrote it. He said he preferred to work on writing at home because he liked to write for longer periods of time than our class period allowed. Working on science was easier at school because he could get it done in smaller amounts of time.

Why should I care when a student completes an assignment so long as the work gets done? This student made an important discovery about his work style and learning preferences and got the job done. Bravo! I need to congratulate this self-starter for his initiative and work ethic. Who am I to demand that only my assignments can be accomplished during my class time? I had to learn to trust students to make the right choices for their own learning and intervene only when they made mistakes.

APPROACH TO THE CURRICULUM

In addition to changing the sequencing of my class period, another major shift I had to make was the way I approached the curriculum. With the new structure, I realized quickly that I couldn't stand up for the entire time and lead students through the lessons. Instead, I needed to include a variety of independent, collaborative, and creative activities to engage students, develop global skills, and promote critical thinking. In one class period, for instance, we had whole-class discussions about *The Great Gatsby*, collaborated in small groups to determine what aspects of current society reflected F. Scott Fitzgerald's view of the American Dream, and worked independently on comparison essays. This variety was critical to maintaining student interest and attention.

One of the key changes I made was how I assessed students. The learning space provided the right atmosphere to implement numerous types of formative assessments. With classroom apps like Socrative, my traditional paper tests and quizzes went online, allowing fast delivery and instant feedback to both students and me about their learning and my teaching. In the conference room connected to my classroom, I was able to meet with students one-on-one for quick check-ins or differentiated writing groups.

Using formative assessments in this way to discuss pending assignments and preview upcoming evaluations reduced test anxiety and created an open environment where students felt comfortable asking questions and discussing their ideas, thereby enabling me to reteach concepts and clear up misunderstandings.

The open learning environment also afforded me more opportunities for performance assessment. Since my traditional tests became my formative assessments, all of my summative assessments were performance and project based. In each of these assessments, I communicated clear learning goals, provided guidelines that incorporated student choice, and developed rubrics that aligned with our learning goals and curriculum standards. One of the best assessments I created was the midterm Graduate Profile presentation. I asked students to prove how they were 21st century global learners, discussing their strengths and weaknesses and providing artifacts that showcased their personal and academic growth both in my English class and in other coursework. Students would sit down one-on-one with me and demonstrate how they were striving to fulfill the Graduate Profile. Students connected deeply with this assignment and had to think critically and creatively as they chose the right artifacts that reflected who they are and the themes they wished to express.

UTILIZING THE LEARNING SPACE

The changes in my approach to curriculum and class time also required a shift in the way I used the learning space. My motto about utilizing the space in Clark Hall was simple: choose your best learning environment. Different instructional activities require different environments. My classroom was the best place for large-group instruction and student presentations. The Common Area where students could be noisy and move around proved the ideal space for interactive activities. The hallways became individual work areas where they could work with fewer distractions. Conference rooms were choice locations for students to work together on group projects.

My haven was the conference room connected to our classroom. This is where I conferenced with individual students and worked with groups on skill development, project check-ins, discussions, and more. In my old classroom, I struggled to work with students individually and in small groups. You would see me in the back of the classroom, conferencing with a student about his writing assignment, struggling to hear him as the classroom noise drowned him out. Clark Hall provided me some peace and quiet to work with kids one-on-one.

(Continued)

(Continued)

Most of the students did very well with this freedom, making responsible choices for the different assignments and activities. Some students liked staying in the classroom to work. Others found their quiet corner in an upstairs hallway away from the rest of the crowd. Others enjoyed working in the Common Area where they could move around. Did students make mistakes? Of course they did. Some students procrastinated and didn't manage their time properly. On occasion, I'd find a sleeping student as I made my rounds. One time I even encountered a student hallway surfing on a rolling ottoman. Students frequently would lose track of time and forget to return to the main classroom at the appointed time. But this issue didn't bother me; students who lost track of time were typically deeply engaged in their work. Surprisingly, I didn't have a single discipline issue the entire year, and student attendance was high. Students, I think, appreciated the freedom, liked the environment, and enjoyed the course so they wanted to be there and show that they could handle the freedom.

TECHNOLOGY

Technology was critical to support these major shifts in my approach to class time, curriculum, and learning spaces. Using technology helped me effectively engage students in a way that made sense to them and met their interactive learning styles. Gen Z digital natives live on social media and know their way around a host of multimedia apps. Participating in an online discussion, listening to an author podcast, and collaborating digitally in the latest classroom app are as natural for students as posting a viral video about a guitar-playing guinea pig.

Not only did technology help engage my students, it also helped keep all of us on the same page. Google Sites, in particular, provided a home base to deliver instruction, communicate information, and monitor progress in a fast and efficient way. Rather than fighting with the copy machine, I used my planning time to build my Google Site, which brought together all of my instructional materials. Each curriculum unit had its own page, full of multimedia resources including e-texts, embedded videos, web links, digital presentations, and more. Old paper handouts became interactive Google Forms, collecting all student responses onto one convenient spreadsheet. Google Sites housed the classroom apps I used to enhance student learning, such as Popplet, Wikispaces, and Turnitin.com. Another advantage to Google Sites is the Hangouts chat feature: with students spread throughout the building, we used chat to locate one another. Having a paperless classroom gave me much of my time back that had previously been spent on classroom management minutia, freeing me to work with students.

AMERICAN EXPERIENCE SHOWCASE

Perhaps the best illustration of the tremendous potential that learning spaces like Clark Hall offer is my end-of-the-year American Experience Showcase. I wanted a project assessment that stretched students and provided them a real audience for their work. Students read a book of their choosing that explored one aspect of the American experience and created interactive displays to showcase to their invited guests for a community book night. I told students to think about their experiences at museums where interacting with the displays is common. Students had about a month and a half to read their book and prepare their displays, which had the following requirements:

- Three original creations (e.g., website, online game, visual display, time lines, artifacts, videos, interviews)

- A visual display (like a tri-board or artifact display)

- One multimedia component

- One connection to your choice book

- A contemporary and/or personal connection (Why is this topic or book relevant?)

- A component of audience interaction (e.g., game, survey)

I provided each student a blank calendar and checklist of steps to complete, which included three conferences with me. Students looked at their own schedules, decided their own due dates for the items on the checklist, and submitted their completed calendars to me. I held students accountable for their own due dates, and the conferences provided me with the assurance that they were making progress. In addition to these preparations, I also tasked students with inviting family and friends to the community book night, requiring each student to bring three people with them and a snack to share.

When trying something new like this community book night, you never know how it will go. I feared only a couple of students showing up (it was outside the regular school day, after all) and presenting to the custodian and me. But the students impressed me. They started setting up their presentations immediately after school and arrived early—with snacks in tow—to make final preparations. The displays and presentations were impressive and powerful. One student recorded and played an original song expressing his opinions about war that he discovered while reading Tim

(Continued)

(Continued)

O'Brien's *The* Things *They Carried*. Another girl created an online quiz to educate visitors about rape with the knowledge she learned while reading Alice Sebold's *Lucky*.

And the guests arrived. Most students exceeded the required number of guests and invited their whole family and group of friends. We encouraged the guests to explore as many displays as they could and talk to students about the books they read. I witnessed students having real conversations with adults about the books they read and the aspect of American experience they explored. One student shared afterward that he spent time talking with a retired social worker who took an interest in his display on child abuse and David Pelzar's book *A Child Called It*, commenting that this discussion provided him a whole new perspective on child abuse. In just one hour, the students experienced something special. A big part of the success of this assignment was the open learning environment; Clark Hall provided the space and time and structure for critical thinking, creativity, collaboration, and communication.

So in the end, are all of these changes worth the time? Absolutely. To any educator wanting to redesign your learning space, I say carpe diem! Tear down those dated motivation posters and think about learning spaces differently. Students need opportunities in open environments to deal with less-structured time so that when they graduate, they are able to manage their future educational environment—whatever it is—and make the right choices to support their own learning. Understand that students may make some wrong choices when they are given this type of freedom. These are lessons all of us have had to learn, and it is probably better to start in high school rather than in college or beyond. Our role as educators is to facilitate this self-discovery and provide students an open leaning environment and opportunities to practice being independent, self-reflective, and global learners. (E. Sturchio, personal communication, May 1, 2015)

Sturchio clearly moved from a disseminator of information to a facilitator of student learning. She adjusted her teaching to fit the needs of the students— she did not force students to adjust their learning to her teaching style. She used the new space as a tool to facilitate learning and to prepare her students to enter a flat world. To accomplish this, she adapted her curriculum, instruction, and assessment to match the learning styles of her 21st century students and the various types of learning space available to them. Her students studied American literature, and she placed a heavy emphasis on creativity, collaboration, and communication. In summary, Sturchio blended a traditional curriculum with global skills and tied her 21st century teaching elements together with technology.

A critical point to remember about this sort of classroom is that it doesn't have to be implemented in one day or even in one year. For our students' sake we must push to move as quickly as we can in our improvement efforts, even to the point of being uncomfortable at times in our growth, but we shouldn't look at an accomplished teacher like Sturchio and say, "Oh, I could never do all of that."

This fundamental questioning does not imply that we must throw everything out and start over; rather, we should question all that we do and keep what works for this century as we embark on one of the greatest transformations in the history of our profession.

IT'S THE TEACHING AND THE RELATIONSHIPS, NOT JUST THE SPACE

Another Clark Hall teacher, Dwayne Marshall, had nearly 30 years of experience teaching social studies when he moved into Clark Hall. He summed up his transition into Clark Hall and teaching Generation Z in this way.

The redesign of my classroom led to such a unique class setting. I was honored that my administration had enough faith in my ability to be creative with student learning that they trusted me. When I was told of the space and of teaching in a 96-minute A/B block, I had to call upon my experience of teaching years before in the Apple Classrooms of Tomorrow (ACOT) where I was placed in a situation where it was okay to try things and most importantly it was okay to fail.

This classroom is part of a new design that is more like a student union than the usual brick and mortar of a public school building. My space today has no traditional desks or chairs. It has a couch, comfortable chairs, two square tables that seat four students as a group, and a bar table with bar chairs, which also seats four students. The room also has a carpet area, ottomans on wheels, and an exercise ball. The room looks more like an upscale waiting room than a traditional classroom!

Adjacent to my room is a small conference room where students can do group work with a full-screen project/smart board. Students have access to several rooms throughout the building as well as a Commons Area, which allows for both individual and group work. All of my students have access to one-on-one technology and the ability to use Google Docs, which allows for both individual and group work. This building requires the students to be

(Continued)

(Continued)

more responsible for their learning and for the teacher to give more control to the students and to better focus on being a student-centered educator.

There are also various areas in the building that allow students to work independently, accomplishing such examples as private reading tasks or working in a small-group discussion. Some rooms are traditional, but the double block A/B schedule dictates that the teaching is not traditional. I teach alone in the classroom, but because of the time schedule and the building, I am in constant collaboration with other teachers in the building. I work closely with the other two government teachers as well with intervention specialists. There is a great deal of sharing of teaching strategies along with immediate help for struggling students who are on Individual Education Plans. One more thing: there are no bells in the building. Students are still expected to be on time.

I can't use a seating chart because of the way the room is designed. I have developed strategies to help me get to know my students by name at the beginning of the year. One of those strategies is developing a short but personal introduction project that helps my students introduce something that is unique about them. Another challenge is planning multiple activities that are relatable to the lesson being taught. I want to make sure that students are engaged and that the classroom and time are being used properly. I also feel that students are engaged in the lesson not only because it is interesting and real world but also because they feel like they are in an atmosphere similar to home.

Does learning take place because of the space or because of the time we devote to it? It is both space and time. My classroom promotes more discussions because the space is more intimate. The space promotes more critical thinking through writing and projects because of the time allotted. What I learned from my students is that they need to be taught how to ask and discuss in-depth questions. They have to learn how to use technology to produce more critical writing as well as learn how to produce better projects. They must learn how to determine group expectations.

I also grew as an educator. I realized that we have to keep in mind that just to change the environment, while not changing the way we teach, will have negative results. We also have to be careful not to believe that just because students know how to use technology, they will do fine in this setting. Students have to be instructed on how to use technology to develop work that is creative and produces critical thinking. Students know how to collaborate, but they still need teacher facilitation to produce an excellent product. To accomplish this, I had to change my assignments. I had to rethink my approach to how to push my students to give me more. I had to do a better job on preparing students for discussions by helping them to ask the right questions. I had to demand better responses from students and myself. The space and the time pushed me to become more rigorous. At the same time, I had to keep the course relative to keep students engaged in the lesson. Most important is that I had to do a better job of building a professional relationship with my students. If students are giving more, it is partly because they trust me. Students tend to produce more if they know I care. (D. Marshall, personal communication, April 27, 2015)

Marshall hit on several key points that all educators must understand as they make their transitions. First, he had the confidence and trust of his administration to try new things and—just as importantly—to occasionally fail. Everyone fails at some point. Some of our greatest growth comes through failure. All of us need second chances, especially when attempting something as complicated as teaching in today's world. He also mentions the importance of redirecting his instruction to help students apply technology and to

▶ Gahanna-Jefferson Public Schools

be successful in small groups. Perhaps most importantly, Marshall stresses the need to develop individual relationships with his students. This goes back to one of the first points presented in this book—the need for trust. There must be trust established among administrators, teachers, and students that all parties have the interests of others in mind as they make decisions.

CLARK HALL TODAY

In Clark Hall today students work online, at the high-top tables in the hallways, on the carpet squares in the classrooms, in the rocking chairs in the common areas, and in the big soft chairs by the huge windows that flood the halls in sunlight. They draw pictures or write fun quotes on the clipboards we hung on the walls.

At the end of the first year, we surveyed students about their new learning space, and they told us, "I learn better in this building . . . I wish all of my classes had been in a building like this! . . . This place is *awesome*!"

We noticed we didn't have many discipline issues in Clark Hall, even with all of the freedom for students to move around. The students and staff seemed more relaxed and focused on teaching and learning. When staff focus too much on rules and restrictions, students feel ruled and restricted. That runs contrary to Generation Z thinking and learning. To teach Generation Z is to set them free with global skills, technology, and flexible learning space.

One student told us, "This building is supposed to be different and help us to be creative. I love it here. It makes me feel creative. I see myself as a little Clark Hall."

Current Gahanna Lincoln High School principal Bobby Dodd summed up the building this way.

> Student learners are evolving much like the teaching methods and resources that are prevalent in schools today. Traditionally in education, while the learners, methods, and resources change, spaces don't. The great part about Clark Hall is that the different types of spaces that exist in the building allow students to learn in a more student-centered, personalized learning environment. Teachers also have the space and resources to instruct and facilitate classes based on preferred learning styles and methods of Generation Z.
>
> In Clark Hall, students work together and collaborate on projects while teachers facilitate the learning and provide assistance when necessary. Many companies and organizations around the world are in need of employees with effective soft skills and the ability to work independently but yet also function on a team. The learning spaces in Clark Hall allow our students to work in this environment and develop these skills that will be beneficial in the future. Clark Hall also provides students and staff with the opportunity to use technology to instruct, assess, and communicate with students. Many teachers use the technology features of the building to incorporate many different types of formative assessment into their daily routines. (B. Dodd, personal communication, June 1, 2015)

▶ Gahanna-Jefferson Public Schools

What began with a few essential questions concluded in a new vision and type of learning space for us. We adopted the attitude that a 21st century learning space is more than a physical space—it's a state of mind. Educators who have visited Clark Hall take the ideas back to their schools—some that have been standing for decades—and they redesign classrooms built 30, 40, and 50 years ago and begin to shift their thinking and their use of space. They realize they don't need to build new buildings to create new types of learning space—they just work with what they have. It might be an entire classroom or perhaps just a corner of a room. They might not have the technology resources of Clark Hall, but they begin to experiment in different ways with what they can muster. They are using their inner mental space to help change how they function in the learning space.

▶ Gahanna-Jefferson Public Schools

Two Essential Questions to Begin the Design of Your Z Space

To evolve in this century, ask questions about fundamental practices. Use the following questions to start the discussion about teaching, learning, and how your fundamental practices relate to the use of learning space.

1. What are the core values of your organization?

2. What kind of learning do you want to see in the new space?

STEP 3

Shift to a 21st Century Teaching Mindset

To begin our transition to creating 21st century learning spaces, we need to realize this shift could be the most difficult and most important adjustment of our careers. Most of us have been trained to think and to act in 20th century models, when students were supposed to sit in straight rows in white classrooms while teachers stood in front of the room and told them what they needed to know to pass a test and move on to the next grade. In earlier, easier times, we could teach the same way our entire careers. A lesson plan created one year was good for 30 years.

But with the advent of the digital age and the changing dynamics of our students, those times are gone and are never coming back. We've all seen the studies and been to professional development sessions where we have been told our students are different today and that they are entering a global workplace where they will need universal skills. They must be able to adapt with an entrepreneurial spirit that will allow them to thrive in the coming decades, whether they live in America, Europe, or Asia or on any other continent.

Most educators want to change. No one wants to be average. No one ever says, "I know I need to adjust my teaching for today's world, but I don't care enough to do it." All educators, deep in their hearts, want to be the best they can be every day for their students. But it's hard today, the most difficult it's ever been, to be a successful American educator. We have test scores that often drive our accountability ratings and teacher assessments, and we have endured severe budget cuts and withering criticism from some of our state and national politicians for not achieving at the high levels they envision (though they often have no accurate view of what educators accomplish daily under some of the most trying of circumstances).

Now, with the rapidly accelerating global economy and the changes we are seeing in our students, the challenge has become even greater. Some days it feels as if we are standing at the base of a steep mountain and wondering how to start the climb to the top. We have heard of the need to teach global skills, incorporate more technology into our teaching, and reinvent learning spaces, but we just don't know where to start or how to do it. Plus, the difficulty of change is increased by the lack of time for training and planning, by the large numbers of students being taught, and by a lack of funding. We could easily say, "This is just too hard. It can't be done." But we won't.

The first step in this climb is a mental one. The world will never stop changing, so we must prepare ourselves for a climb that will never end. How we teach at the end of our careers could be very different from how we are teaching now. To have the strength and fortitude to make the shift to this mindset of constant change and improvement, we must remember why we became teachers. Whether it was last year or in the previous century, we did it because we wanted to help young people, as if we heard a voice inside our hearts calling us to be teachers. Only educators can understand it. We must tap into the passion we felt for wanting to make our part of the world a better place, because that is the greatest force to drive educators. That passion will help us to endure the challenges ahead.

The shift to a 21st century mindset is a challenge that must be accepted daily. The teaching of global skills and the implementation of student technology cannot just be incorporated into curriculum units that are taught once in the fall and once in the spring—they must be daily, fundamental parts of our classroom instruction. Change begins with us. It must begin immediately.

We must ensure that we are looking at teaching and learning from a 21st century perspective, not one from the 20th century. New learning spaces, whether they are in new buildings or redesigned classrooms, should be designed around a new way of thinking that brings in new sources, has new goals, and has the flexibility to be adjusted in the coming decades as learning styles continue to evolve and global skills are redefined.

To begin the process of reshaping our space, here are 15 important points to guide us.

VIEW SPACE REDESIGN AS A K–12 PROCESS

For many years, primary grade level teachers have used space effectively in their classrooms as they have developed stations, differentiated instruction, and integrated their subjects. These practices are more important than ever and must continue, even as teachers in early grades come under increasing pressure with standardized testing. Teachers at the middle school and high school levels should adopt some of the philosophies of the elementary schools and use their learning space more creatively. Students should be able to go through school from kindergarten to the 12th grade and see a common effort made at using space to meet the needs of the learner.

UNDERSTAND THAT SPACE REDESIGN CAN BE DONE ON A LARGE OR SMALL SCALE

Some schools are fortunate enough to be able to redesign an entire wing or to design a new school, but in most cases the redesign efforts will begin on a small scale in one or two classrooms. Sometimes the rooms might be in buildings that are 50, 60, or even 100 years old. Although it would help to have a new building, we must be resourceful with what we have.

FIND WAYS TO MAKE THIS SHIFT EVEN WHEN BUDGETS ARE TIGHT

Only a handful of schools in the world have an unlimited budget with which to redesign learning space. Educators with small budgets can begin with one corner of a classroom, an entire classroom, or a few classrooms. A space redesign can begin with something as simple as using a donated carpet and a few soft chairs.

Here are some tips for finding resources to begin the process of redesigning space in a classroom or in one part of a school when there's not much money available through the school or district to purchase paint, carpeting, furniture, technology, or anything else you envision in the new space. (If you are a teacher, check with your administration first to make sure you have its support as you solicit money or other donations.)

- Ask the PTO if it has any funds to support your space redesign.

- Perhaps you know a local business owner who supports education at the local level and would be willing to help fund it. Maybe you know of several benevolent donors. If several of them donated modest amounts of money then it could quickly add up. Again, a lot can be done in a classroom with several hundred dollars.

- Go to specific paint stores, furniture stores, or other merchants who specialize in products for which you are searching and see if they have any local or national corporate programs for education donations.

- Try to find some parents who are progressive in their thinking and would be willing to donate material or to fund purchases.

(Continued)

(Continued)

- Look for grants at the local, state, and national level that foster new ways of thinking and educating young people.

- Ask your friends to spread the word that you are trying something new in your school or classroom, and see if any of them would be willing to help.

- Be sure to ask anyone who helps you if they, too, would ask their friends to also be of assistance.

- Use social media. One librarian who is featured later in this book (Ann Gleek) asked her Facebook friends to help her by posting this message:

Hi friends – I need some help. I am looking for things to be donated to the GLHS library to help me create a makerspace. So, if you have any old Legos, Tinker Toys, Circuit sets, or anything along those lines that you no longer need, PLEASE send me a message!!! (A. Gleek, personal communication, August 7, 2015)

- If your school is willing to make a long-term plan for space redesign, make it a highly visible goal that could be funded through the PTO, fund-raisers, and other ways it accrues money from outside sources.

GET TECHNOLOGY INTO THE HANDS OF OUR STUDENTS, EVEN WHEN THERE ARE OBSTACLES

We must find a way to look beyond the problem to see what we need to do. In other words, instead of dwelling on the fact that we don't have enough devices for all of our students or that the current technology system can't support the computers or often crashes, we need to say, "We might not have the system we want, but how can we use what we have?"

BUILD A CULTURE OF TRUST IN OUR SCHOOLS

True education progress in which the administrators, teachers, students, parents, and community move together toward common goals requires that all parties treat each other with respect and that all parties show understanding and kindness. Communication must be clear, honest, and focused on achieving the prescribed goals. Politics and egos should be pushed aside, and the mission of educating young people must be the top priority.

RECOGNIZE THAT A LEARNING SPACE CAN ENHANCE 21st CENTURY LEARNING

It's scary to do something different, but we must be brave. We must dream of what the space can be and how it can positively affect learning. Educators are extremely bright and imaginative professionals. A space redesign project is an opportunity to bring out the most creative ideas in educators, students, and community members. Each project has unique challenges depending on the vision, goals, history, personalities, politics, and finances of the environment. The work we do today prepares us for rapid improvement tomorrow.

Another district that has used its space to meet the needs of Generation Z is Hilliard City Schools in Ohio. When the district created a new type of environment for some of its students who wanted to learn in nontraditional ways, it constructed the Hilliard McVey Individual Learning Center (ILC). Brent Wise is its director.

Many of the spaces we have designed at the ILC promote collaboration and communication not only among students currently enrolled in the same class but in different classes. We believe students will be enriched to have conversations across disciplines, much like a college student union. We want outsiders to not know what classes are taking place, just students creating and learning together. Students can move freely from space to space. We have a 10-80-10 philosophy. The first 10% of class the teacher engages the students, the 80% middle portion of class the students own the learning and move about the space, and the final 10% of class the students come back together and the teacher assesses their understanding and sets the stage for tomorrow's learning.

The ILC is built around student voice and choice in the curriculum. We offer students four networks to plug into to find a course or experience that interests them. The networks are College Jumpstart, Personal Success, Imagination, and Young Professionals. If students are interested in sound engineering we offer a recording studio rock band course. If students are interested in television production we offer students a media communication course in our green screen studio. Students that are interested in the medical profession, education, or business are able to experience authentic mentorships during their high school years. This and many more offer our students real-world experiences.

Technology has become part of what we do. The devices we provide are simply a tool that students use to create and enhance the learning

(Continued)

(Continued)

experience that is designed for them by the teacher. The authentic experience is designed not with the technology in mind but rather with the learning outcome in mind. The technology is simply the tool used to enhance that experience and tell the story if applicable.

Freedom has worked. Giving students ownership of a space and raising expectations. We have redesigned a space several times because students like this or don't like that. (B. Wise, personal communication, April 14, 2015)

A Flexible Building for Grades 2–8

The New Albany Plain Local School District recently opened a building that houses students in Grades 2–8, and its superintendent, Dr. April Domine, stressed from the beginning of the building's design stages that a different thought process needed to be employed and the space had to be flexible enough to meet the needs of today's students.

When climbing enrollment resulted in buildings that were overcrowded, the New Albany Plain Local Schools faced the need to build a new building. The vision of the district is to "be the leader in reinventing education," and this vision created the opportunity to build a building that would reinvent how space could be designed to encourage the future of education. Fundamental to the concept driving the design was the expectation that every space should do three things, and therefore the space must be able to flex into whatever the teacher and student may need to do. This resulted in learning communities with classrooms with movable, writeable walls with transparent movable garage doors and windows into small conference rooms as well as a center core to the building with flexible STEM and messy labs and small café-style areas that double as learning spaces. In each community, the classrooms center around learning commons that provide flexible spaces and furnishings that can easily move and change for large groups, small groups, and independent work that ranges from quiet work, to public presentations, to project-based messy work, to collaborative teamwork. The transparency of walls and large garage door openings facilitates a sense of ongoing community, teamwork, and independence. From a safety and supervision point of view, the teachers and students can see everyone in the learning community and their work. Vibrant colors, furniture on wheels, and soft furniture that moves easily purposefully inspire those in the space to be energized to be independent and creative; students take responsibility to manage their work and engage in independent as well as project-based collaborative work.

The design process was highly collaborative and involved multiple stakeholders and numerous opportunities for input. The work began with a community and staff Facility Advisory Committee. This group began the work with the superintendent's guidance to learn about how space is used in a variety of educational and corporate spaces (such as Google) to facilitate the type of learning and work that reflects the collaboration, teamwork, and creative problem solving that is essential to work in the future. The group focused on how space is a tool for learning and not simply a grouping of typical educational spaces. With a focus on the purpose of space to foster learning, the group then learned from new student-centered learning guidelines for schools from the Ohio School Facility Commission and their lead architect, Kevin Harrison. In this research the group learned that student-centered spaces are even more cost effective than typical construction. The group then created a budget for the building before the design had even begun to demonstrate to the community that a budget could be set based on all the other buildings on campus, including the size of the building needed and the cost per square foot. The design then was continually held to the standard of building a student-centered, flexible learning environment for the same cost or less than what it would take to build a traditional school that was a replica of existing buildings.

▶ Mark White

(Continued)

(Continued)

From the very beginning, the community, staff, and students were invited to participate in design sessions on continually evolving drafts for the building's shape and form. The architectural firm led charettes with multiple designs in a variety of open community forums, gathering what people loved and hated about the exterior to create the outside form and what they aspired for the space to provide. From these sessions came great feedback about how to make the outside of the building fit on the campus and also include outdoor learning spaces. Input from environmental science teachers led to a greenhouse, green roofs, and amphitheatre-style green spaces between the building labs to bring outdoor learning directly into the labs. The inside form was designed to focus on educational purpose and create learning communities with flexibility and transparency with open common collaborative space, smaller conference rooms for small-group work, collaborative office space for teachers, and flexible STEM and messy lab spaces with a smaller, more intimate, café-like eating experience. Feedback from students, staff, parents, and community members, as well as the Facility Advisory Committee, continually shaped the design.

▶ April Domine

The first wing of the building opened in the fall of 2014 and provided an essential opportunity to test and learn from the use of the space. Students took to the space intrinsically and are highly productive as they spread out and use the space flexibly as it has been designed. One of the challenges is the reaction of adults, parents, and staff to the space. For community

members, we continually stressed the budget-driven process based on the cost of replicating the existing building with a focus on creating the workplace of the future. Many business leaders reinforce this when they visit. They remark that the space emulates much of what they are trying to create in the workplace with visible collaboration and flexible shared spaces to foster teamwork and problem solving. The space has a dramatic impact on the work of both students and staff. It fosters the collaboration, flexibility, and self-directed nature of work that is highly engaging. We have more to learn about what works and what doesn't. We did learn a great deal in the first phase opening, and I would highly recommend small-space conversions leading up to a full building design and furniture purchase. For space to simply be a tool for learning, staff must continually have the opportunity to learn about how approaches to self-directed, collaborative, team-based problem solving and creative work can be infused into any content. These opportunities to explore pedagogy, combined with exposure to new space, can be transformational not only for students but for those who lead them to learn every day.
(A. Domine, personal communication, August 9, 2015)

Domine says the building is also different in other ways: "We highlighted the waste in typical design—large lobby spaces and long double-loaded corridors equal square footage that could be used for educational purpose . . . [and the district wanted to] avoid the waste of cafeterias that sit empty except during lunch time . . . and every space must do three things" (A. Domine, personal communication, August 9, 2015).

Domine also highlights the challenges of moving into the space such as

> helping adults find courage to explore and use the space. Students take to it immediately and use it as intended. Ongoing encouragement for staff is needed and is provided by early innovators regarding movable walls. One of the greatest challenges for staff was the need to hang things on walls—when all are usable—some wipe-off spaces and movable walls using them like fixed unwriteable walls. Parents indicated that the collaborative commons or transparent walls would be too much a distraction for their student and even parents of ADHD and anxiety-disorder students have since indicated that the space had the reverse effect on them, that in fact they were more attentive and focused on their work. (A. Domine, personal communication, August 9, 2015)

MAKE THE SPACE REDESIGN A GROUP EFFORT

In a simplified look at 20th century school leadership, most superintendents made sure the budget was balanced, ensured the principals were hired, tried to keep the school buses running on schedule, and handled any societal or personal problems that came their way from the principals or parents. Those issues are still confronted by all school leaders, but the scope of a superintendent's job has become much broader. School leaders today, including principals at all levels, deal with a vast range of accountability measures; the magnification of issues through the lens of the local press and social media; the importance of school security; increasing scrutiny from state and local politicians; and the task of transforming an often overburdened system into a globally competitive organization. Is it any wonder so many reform efforts fail? With all of the requirements facing today's school leaders, the only way schools will survive in this century is through sincere efforts to distribute leadership throughout the district and school. No school leader can do it alone, regardless of level or leadership abilities. The scope of the task and other job requirements is too immense.

A key shift in the fundamental approach to 21st century learning must occur early in the process and carry through all the way to the assessment of student learning: *we must view our students as our partners, not just the isolated parties at the end of the delivery system.* Shouldn't the people for whom we are designing the building have a voice in its design? We must seek constant feedback from our students in all that we do in schools, especially in this time of rapid change as we seek to catch up with their learning styles and with their demands. Students can provide valuable feedback on how they like to learn, what they find interesting, and what they want to see in a new learning space. This idea does not have to be restricted to high school students, but middle school students and some elementary students can also provide keen insight for adults as to what will work in a new type of learning space.

Talk to students, parents, and staff about what they observe in local coffee shops, sandwich places, and other social spaces used for gathering, meetings, and brainstorming. Daniel Pink wrote in his foreword to the book *The New Social Learning* by Tony Bingham and Marcia Conner, "In so many ways, learning is a social act. From circle time in kindergarten, to study groups in college, to team projects in the workforce, sociability has always greased the gears of learning."

In promoting student leadership on our committees, surveys, or other redesign activities, we gain valuable input and instill a tremendous global skill in them: the skill of leadership. Student participation in this initiative could profoundly transform both the school and the students' lives. Shaping leadership is an art, and a school redesign initiative can allow students who were not originally thought of as leaders to emerge as powerful allies. As we seek out the identified leaders, we should also search for those who have the untapped potential to blossom into leaders.

Ask what the leadership role of teachers will be in this initiative. We must determine if a teacher will be coleader with an administrator and if teachers can lead other parts of the initiative. Fellow teachers often have inventive ideas, and they can be strong partners in providing ideas and helping to explain the purpose and process to others. Our teachers are often waiting to lead. Every school has teachers who are natural leaders and have formal titles such as grade level leader, head of department, or department chair. These educators must be involved and helping to lead space redesign efforts. In addition, schools have informal teacher leaders who have great ideas but don't hold official titles. They, too, can play critical roles. It's up to the administrator to find them and to include them.

If we provide opportunities for parents to provide feedback during the design stages, they will be more likely to understand and accept the changes. Some of them will have positive ideas that bring improvements. Work with an already established group such as the PTO or PTA or launch a Parent Advisory Board to include parent voice and support. All parents want to feel connected to their schools, and involving them in this important redesign process will provide benefits to students, educators, and parents that range beyond this one initiative.

In addition, people who work outside of education often are interested in new ideas in education and like to be a part of the transformation. This group could include local business people, vendors, local politicians, and various other community members and leaders. Everyone cares about the quality of the local schools and wants to be involved in movements that will have a positive, deep impact on the learning of their community's young people. In addition, these external partners can often bring expertise, services, monetary or material donations, and reduced costs to the project.

BE COMFORTABLE WITH BEING UNCOMFORTABLE

Strong teachers have strong opinions. One of the guiding forces that pushes educators to greatness is a passion for helping young people. When those educators enter into discussions on curriculum, assessment, school policies, or space redesign, it's only natural that those opinions and passions emerge in multiple ways, from the research they do to ideas they offer in group discussions. However, a passion for improvement is a double-edged sword: if it is controlled then it can be hugely beneficial; however, if some educators are inflexible or overly assertive, they can slow the initiative's progress. The leaders of the group must find ways to tap into strong opinions and passions without allowing them to overwhelm the group.

Just as important, all members of a space redesign team must understand that new ways of teaching and using space will bring a natural uncertainty that can be unsettling for professionals who have been comfortable and extremely competent in their traditional roles. A certain amount of uncertainty can be a positive element. Growth in individuals and organizations often occurs when they step out of their comfort zones and branch into new, uncharted areas. Embrace the uncertainty. We should step to the edge of our comfort and then walk beyond its boundaries.

STUDY WHAT RESEARCHERS ARE
SAYING ABOUT 21ST CENTURY LEARNING

Read the work of authors such as Ian Jukes, Yong Zhou, Tony Wagner, Thomas Friedman, Daniel Pink, Chip and Dan Heath, Alfie Kohn, Sal Khan, Malcolm Gladwell, and Seth Godin. They have spent much of their careers studying changes in the global marketplace and suggesting changes that should be made in teaching and learning. They repeatedly stress global skills, learning styles, and access to technology.

GATHER IDEAS FROM NEW SOURCES

Study the workspace of high-tech firms and contemporary offices and the learning spaces of modern university libraries. Some companies and universities have already redesigned some of their space to foster freedom of thought and creative thinking. Research the working space of the most creative companies in the world (think Silicon Valley high-tech companies!). If there are any new office spaces in nearby large cities, try to see if they have incorporated any new features. Take tours of a university library that has been recently remodeled. The odds are its space will look different and function in different ways from the libraries of the 20th century.

Google the images for work spaces of companies such as Google; Intel; Pixar; New Tech High Network schools; Skullcandy International Office in Zurich, Switzerland; BBC North in Manchester, England; iProspect in Fort Worth, Texas; and Case Rex in Brazil, to name a few. You will notice a focus on collaboration and the use of natural light, open space, and flexible furniture.

Talk with a local architect or tour a new office building and notice what has been done with furniture, lighting, color, hallways, walls, artwork, collaborative space, and technology.

Go online and see what universities are doing with learning space today. Many of our Generation Z graduates will matriculate into American universities, and when they do, a number of them could encounter new types of spaces designed specifically to fit their needs. University librarians across America are realizing that they need to adapt to this generation and its needs, and a number of them have taken steps that include removing some of the book stacks and adding more comfortable furniture and various types of rooms and spaces that can be used for different purposes. The same efforts have been applied to university student centers; the traditional student hangouts of the past are being transformed into environments that cater to Generation Z.

An example may be found at Ohio Dominican University (ODU) in Columbus, Ohio. The university has an enrollment of over 2,000 students and prides itself on being a Catholic liberal arts school that prepares its students in the Dominican tradition. Several years ago when it constructed the Bishop James A. Griffin Student Center, ODU knew it had to create a new type of space for its Generation Z students. The result is a popular building filled with different types of spaces, comfortable furniture, and massive windows that look out onto trees and a nearby creek.

▶ Photo © George C. Anderson

▶ Photo © George C. Anderson

For more examples, go online and look at images of The Ohio State University library and The Ohio State University Student Union, two recently renovated spaces that are now among the best in the world. Others include buildings at the University of Wisconsin-Madison and the University of Chicago. They recognized the need to redesign their learning environments to meet the needs of today's students by creating learning space outside the walls of the lecture hall, library cubicles, and classrooms.

FORM CLEAR OBJECTIVES FOR HOW WE WANT TO USE THE SPACE AND COMMUNICATE THOSE OBJECTIVES TO OUR STAFF AND COMMUNITY

A new learning space should be designed around global skills, the learning styles of 21st century students, and how students will use technology to create new products. This means there will be rooms specifically designed for various purposes, which could lead to variations in furniture selection, room sizes, paint colors, technology acquisitions, natural lighting considerations, and possible future needs—which could all be new concepts for a community to ponder.

When offering new ideas to a group of students, educators, parents, and community members, remember that the group can often be split into three sections. The first section, the most imaginative one, will be fully supportive and excited about the potential of the new type of space to affect learning. The second section, which will probably be the largest one, will probably be made up of people who don't have strong opinions but are willing to support the redesign process if the school has a history of success and transparency. On the other hand, if the school has a negative history with the group then this middle section of people will tend to be pessimistic in its view of the redesign process. Finally, almost all new ideas, especially if they are radical, draw criticism from a section that wishes to maintain the status quo. These people were successful in the traditional system; a common quote will be, "The old way worked for me so it's good enough for today's kids." A question to ask is, "But how much better could it have been if you had been exposed to a different opportunity?"

As we shift our thinking to these points, we must move beyond the "yeahbuts." Many times someone in a school might have a good idea for improvement, but someone else will quickly say, "Yeah, but we tried that once," or "Yeah, but we don't have the money for that," or "Yeah, but our technology doesn't work," or "Yeah, but that would never work here." These are the yeahbuts. We must not let them stop us. Educators could cover an entire wall with reasons not to try something new, but on the opposite wall could be written one sentence: "We have to keep trying because our students are worth it." Just because an earlier initiative failed doesn't mean that all future ones will also be unsuccessful. History is filled with organizations that learned from their mistakes, refocused their efforts, and found ways to climb to new levels.

EMBRACE SOCIAL MEDIA

We should let people know what we are doing with learning space and why we are doing it. People don't always hear all of the information or understand new ideas the first time they are heard, so it's imperative that we have multiple avenues of communication. Some people will still go to a school website for information, but many people today get their information from social media sites on their cell phones. Use more than the school website; use Twitter, Facebook, YouTube, Google+, or Vimeo videos to share your school or district's story.

Identify key people in the organization who have a strong social media presence, who can provide advice and help to disseminate the information via their followers and online friends. The time to build a professional social network is *before* the redesign process begins so that the lines of communication are already established. It's also helpful to spread information quickly and accurately. In today's social media world, the absence of official information invites noninformed individuals to spread inaccurate information, and once this happens it becomes difficult to clarify the misconceptions.

CONSIDER THE FINISHING TOUCHES FIRST

In the building of most traditional schools, there is a time late in the planning stages when the interior paint colors are chosen, the furniture is selected, the type of windows is decided, and the technology infrastructure is added. In most schools, the paint colors are mild colors that fit the tastes of adults and are the same ones that have been used for many years. The individual student desks, which are often slight variations of desks used 100 years ago, are often purchased in bulk and are disseminated equally in all classrooms. The windows, which allow rooms to be illuminated by natural lighting, are afterthoughts or reduced in size in the hopes of reducing visual access into the room or making a forced entry more difficult. The technology infrastructure, from the servers to the wireless ports, are usually provided at a level barely sufficient to serve the students and staff when the building initially opens, with little or no capacity built in for additional growth in the future.

By contrast, in a 21st century learning space, these areas should be among the first considered, and their importance should be elevated. School designers should consider alternative colors, and the students should choose some of them. Also, this is not the 1950s—some school colors are fine, but a school today doesn't need to have its school colors everywhere. School spirit is a feeling and a culture, not just a color on the wall. In today's world we must keep security in mind, but we should also remember that large windows allow natural lighting to contribute to a positive environment and can reduce heating costs. Technology is the foundation of most 21st century learning, and it will continue to grow in importance. It should be at the center of all space redesign.

ACKNOWLEDGE THAT THE LEARNING SPACE IS ONLY AS GOOD AS THE TEACHING THAT TAKES PLACE IN IT

Building a new learning space will not automatically improve teaching and learning. For a century, educators have sometimes made the mistake of thinking a new building will solve teaching and assessment issues. It will not. It's not the room or the space that makes a great classroom; it's the quality of the teacher. If a new space is created without thoroughly training the teachers moving into the space, then they will take their 20th century models with them. Better teaching is a result of better training, and new learning spaces call for new practices and personalized, progressive professional development.

Teachers are highly intelligent, skilled professionals, and planning effective training for them is extremely difficult because they have such high standards. To prepare teachers to transition into a space in which they can focus on teaching global skills, tailor their teaching to fit the needs of their 21st century students, and make technology the foundation of their instruction, their training must model what we hope to see in their classrooms. We must train teachers by listening to their requests and tailoring our instruction to fit their learning needs. One size does not always fit all individuals when it comes to training. We must consult with teachers on the goals and pacing and ask what we can do to make the instruction interesting and pertinent. We must release them at appropriate times to learn on their own or with others, including small groups of subject- or grade-level teachers. Teachers must be free to create new products, and we must give them opportunities and venues to display their learning and to help others to learn and to explore new ideas. The technology teachers use must be fast, reliable, and supported by a strong system. We must be risk takers and encourage our teachers to be risk takers. The instruction should be available in a mixed format where some of it is delivered in a classroom or meeting room and some of it is available online 24/7.

Before we can grasp this type of professional development, we must let go of the 20th century notions of control, of strict deadlines for learning, of an inflexible professional development curriculum, and of the idea that all teachers will be in the same spot in their development at the end of the training. Individuals develop at their own rate. We must provide follow-up support that allows all teachers to continue their growth and lays the foundation for future development.

EMBRACE THE IDEA THAT THE TEACHER IN A 21ST CENTURY LEARNING SPACE WILL BE A FACILITATOR, NOT THE DISSEMINATOR OF INFORMATION

Up until this point in history, the teacher possessed all the knowledge the student would need to pass a subject. The teacher controlled the elements of the textbook to be taught, the pacing of the curriculum, and the type of assessment given to students. However, the advent of the information age means textbooks can be relegated to a support role as students use the Internet to gather research. Teachers will still play a vital role; all students will continue to need great teachers to guide them, to help them to assess their progress, and to ensure a high level of learning is occurring. However, the exponential growth of knowledge in this century means the teacher should no longer be the main disseminator of information. Instead, the teacher must develop a different type of skill set centered on the Internet and student devices, the types of global skills needed in a global economy, and the learning characteristics of 21st century young people. We must think of it this way: our students today are entering a world evolving more rapidly than ever before, and their world of 30 or 40 years into the future will require skills that we can only imagine—they will be using the descendants of the global skills we teach them today. From this point forward, for teachers to be truly effective they must transition to a facilitator's role.

PROFESSIONAL DEVELOPMENT ACTIVITIES TO SHIFT THINKING TO A 21ST CENTURY MINDSET

Collaborate

- Determine if there is a level of trust in your school that will allow students, teachers, and administrators to think freely, to express themselves, and to implement new ideas.

- Discuss ways to express opinions without creating confrontation.

- Establish the ways students, staff, parents, and community members can participate in the redesign process.

Think Critically

- Discuss why some teachers make successful transitions to new teaching styles and others don't. Determine the keys to helping teachers to shift to a 21st century teaching model and break down the barriers.

- Read a website or blog by a futurist such as Sir Ken Robinson, Ian Jukes, Seth Godin, Malcolm Gladwell, or Thomas Friedman to learn about the trends of the last decade and what they mean for future developments. Search the web for progressive teaching rubrics and tailor them to fit the needs of your school.

- Watch several TEDTalks about the brain, creativity, global skills, innovation, risk taking, and the future of education and jot down several key takeaways that can be used to discuss with colleagues.

Create

- Work with others to form a list of books, articles, websites, and other sources that help teachers to understand more about 21st century learning.

- Do a book study with other educators and discuss the book's themes and their implications for learning in your classroom.

- If money is available, devote a day of professional development to a nationally known speaker who can address 21st century trends. If money is not available, see if any local professors or civic leaders can address the staff on a topic pertaining to the global economy, the need for competitive skills, or international business trends and how they are affecting the local area.

- Work with students and other staff members to create a video on the school's vision and challenges.

- Discuss with staff members what role 21st century teaching ideas should play in educator assessment.

Communicate

- Begin to form clear talking points you can use to describe your space redesign.

- Make a list of all the ways you will communicate with students, staff, parents, and the community.

- Determine your number of social media contacts and search for ways to enlarge it.

- Ask one or two members of the redesign team who are highly proficient in social media to coordinate the social media communication efforts.

- Create a bulletin board in a prominent area of the school where teachers and students can share their ideas about 21st century learning with each other and with visitors.

- Create a blog that shares ideas and questions, share it with others, and invite feedback.

- Create a Twitter account just for this project and share it with others. As ideas occur, they can be tweeted 24/7.

- Develop a Facebook page where people can post ideas, photos, and links.

- Participate in a weekly Twitter chat such as #edchat or #satchat to get ideas from other innovative educators about school redesign for student learning.

- Create an Instagram account to post pictures of creative and innovative learning spaces to share with colleagues or committee members.

Stretch to the Future

- Determine the 20th century habits that need to be replaced in 21st century professional development.

- Find the edge of your comfort zone and look for ways to slowly expand it. Search for new ideas that make you feel uncomfortable because they are so different from your normal thinking and delve into them to see if they warrant more inspection.

- Ensure that your professional development models what you want to see in your classrooms.

- Set aside a time each week to study change individually or to discuss transformational ideas as a group.

- Form an idea of what teaching will look like in the future and begin to establish your own path for transitioning from a disseminator of information to a facilitator of knowledge.

- Examine the role of grades in the 21st century classroom. Ask if grades are needed, if they motivate or demotivate students, and if they are still the most accurate ways of showing what students have learned.

- Discuss the ways schools are assessed today and ask if there are more accurate ways to determine the success of students, educators, and entire schools in the 21st century.

- Think of the features commonly found in 20th century schools and determine which of them are still relevant today and which ones need to be changed.

- Host an unconference, or open conference, in which the participants set the agenda of ideas. Center it on school redesign to spark discussion and to promote collaborative, creative thinking. Decide on action steps and then move forward.

Think of the strengths and weaknesses of your school or classroom culture and determine ways to improve trust and risk taking.

Create a list of students, staff members, parents, and community members who will participate in the redesign process and identify their roles.

Identify the 21st century mindset ideas the design team (or school or community) will most easily accept and those with which it will struggle.

STEP 4

Teach Global Skills

If a teacher who retired in 1995 walked into a classroom today, would that teacher see the exact same type of teaching and classroom design he or she had used in 1995? Or would it be a different one?

One hopes that retired teacher would see a classroom where young people were using their minds to create new ideas. Thomas Friedman recently quoted Tony Wagner in the *New York Times*: "The capacity to innovate— the ability to solve problems creatively or bring new possibilities to life—and skills like critical thinking, communication and collaboration are far more important than academic knowledge" (Friedman, 2013).

It must be stressed that a new type of learning space will not guarantee an improvement in learning unless we adopt a 21st century teaching philosophy and use the space differently. Although some teachers have successfully made the shift to a 21st century teaching style, many teachers continue to struggle, partly because of forces beyond their control.

STANDARDIZED TESTING AND GLOBAL SKILLS

A huge reason many of our schools have not made this shift is because our teachers have been focused on state-mandated standardized testing. Our emphasis has been on being successful within the borders of our states, not in a world without borders. This is not to say these tests are not useful or important. First, they help to measure some of the core academic skills our students need to master. Our students must be able to read, to write, to function in math, and to understand essential concepts in science and history. Standardized tests have continued to evolve and to push more higher-level thinking skills. Of course, we know another reason these tests are important is that they are the standard by which our students and schools are measured. We want our students to do well for their sake, and we want our schools to be respected. We must continue to prepare our students for their standardized assessments.

But for our students to be globally competitive, they must do more than be successful on their state tests. They must sharpen their skills in the 4 C's, which means we must stress creativity, communication, and collaboration

("P21 Common Core Toolkit") and ask students to do more critical thinking than is needed to do well on the standardized assessments.

Thus, we have two tracks in front of us: one that promotes standardized testing and one that promotes 21st century learning and global skills. Our first response might be to say that these tracks are two distinct, parallel paths that cannot be merged and that our efforts must be directed down the path of standardized testing because that is the path on which we and our students will be held accountable. However, we must find a way to merge these paths, to prepare our students to excel on their tests while also giving them the skills they need to display their knowledge in new and creative ways. This is difficult because whereas a few professional development initiatives might stress the importance of global skills, the majority of our efforts have been dedicated to raising test scores. Some state and national leaders espouse the need for our students to have global skills, yet they often mandate more standardized testing. In addition, the assessment models used for teachers, administrators, and districts continue to place a growing emphasis on test scores. This means efforts at moving beyond the state tests must often begin when the individual teacher, school, or district takes the initiative to do so. In other words, we must maintain a part of the world we already understand and create a new part at the same time while under extreme pressure to excel in the old model. Is it any wonder it's been so difficult to do? How many professions can accomplish such a transformation?

One of the first steps in implementing global skills is to determine the type of global skills to be presented in a curriculum and the terminology to be used. At this point in our educational development, there is unfortunately no set list of the required skills to teach, nor is there a common terminology. For example, some of us might say that students must "think at high levels" whereas another group of educators might say students must be able to "think critically." Some teachers promote creativity whereas others promote entrepreneurship. It would be helpful to all educators in the organization if a common terminology could be determined. But because there is no master list that crosses over state or district lines, these terms can be developed within each organization.

THE COMMON CORE STATE STANDARDS

The majority of educators in America now use the Common Core State Standards (CCSS), so it could be a good place to start for those who are already teaching them ("About the Standards"). But instead of viewing them through the lens of a mandated curriculum that leads to high-stakes student testing and teacher assessment, let's view them as vehicles through which to teach global skills. A principal goal of the Common Core is to make America more competitive through the implementation of skills. We could debate the merit of the standardized assessments, the volume of assessments, and other aspects of the CCSS implementation, but if we look closely we can find a number of global skill threads running through the CCSS, and these could be starting points for discussion.

How deeply do the CCSS skills go? A study by Achieve found that a number of global skills are "strongly/largely reflected in the CCSS." The skills include "communication skills . . . teamwork/collaboration skills . . . problem solving skills . . . reasoning skills . . . application/extension of core content . . . use of data . . . research skills . . . time management skills . . . [and] use of technology." Other skills could be closely aligned or could be easily brought into the CCSS framework. However, the study concludes that the CCSS do not cover every skill that students need, nor were the CCSS meant to cover them. Whereas the CCSS are meant to help a student to be college and career ready, they are not meant to be all-encompassing for success in the 21st century. There are a number of skills cited by Achieve as not being present, such as "conflict resolution . . . technology-based project management skills . . . [and] ethical reasoning" ("Understanding the Skills in the Common Core State Standards").

It must also be noted that the CCSS only represent mathematics and the language arts, and other standard sets must be brought into the curriculum for other subjects. So, if we are already using the CCSS, then some of the skills could be present in our curriculum, but we would need to delve deeper to create a more encompassing set.

Some states in America have opted out of the CCSS, and educators in those states will find similarities in their standards with CCSS and the standards used in other states. They can go through the same process as educators using the CCSS. They can begin their skills effort by searching for the global skills in their standards and forming a list of strengths and weaknesses.

OTHER SOURCES FOR GLOBAL SKILLS

To move beyond the set curriculum and create a deeper list of skills, a teacher, school, or district must decide if it is going to create its own list or save time and energy by adopting the skills and terminology of nationally known entities that have spent years developing and promoting them. Some of these entities have membership opportunities available, for a fee, which could assist the district in training and implementation.

There are a number of companies and organizations from which to choose. One of the most popular global skills initiatives is the Partnership for 21st Century Skills, also known as P21. Schools that join the framework gain access to its resources and its efforts to implement skills in the areas of "life and career skills . . . learning and innovation skills—4 C's . . . information, media, and technology skills . . . core subjects—3 R's, and 21st century themes." Though some of the P21 skills can be found in the CCSS, the P21 framework offers other skills such as "civic literacy . . . health literacy . . . environmental literacy . . . media literacy . . . initiative and self direction . . . social and cross cultural skills . . . [and] productivity and accountability" ("P21 Common Core Toolkit").

The Global Digital Citizen Foundation offers a set of 21st Century Fluencies that include "solution fluency . . . creativity fluency . . . collaboration fluency . . . media fluency . . . [and] information fluency." It breaks the fluencies into subcategories with action headings such as "ask . . . analyze . . . [and] assess" skills in the information fluency and "establish . . . envision . . . execute . . . [and] engineer" skills in the collaboration fluency (21st Century Fluencies | Global Digital Citizen Foundation).

The Metiri Group assists schools in implementing skills in the areas of "digital age literacy . . . inventive thinking . . . effective communication . . . [and] high productivity." Some of its skills include "curiosity, creativity, and risk taking . . . visual and information literacies . . . [and] personal, social and civic responsibility" ("EnGauge 21st Century Skills").

EdLeader 21 assists schools in implementing the 4 C's of communication, collaboration, critical thinking, and creativity. They call themselves the "professional learning community for 21st century ed. leaders" and provide free downloads of useful resources. The bulk of their services comes with becoming a member ("The Professional Learning Community for 21st Century Education Leaders").

A number of nationally known authors such as Thomas Friedman, Ian Jukes, Tony Wagner, Seth Godin, and Daniel Pink have explored the need for global skills, and each has written extensively about the need to reform what we teach and to view the world through a global lens. Their work, too, can be a valuable resource and provide stepping-off points for staff discussions.

Just as importantly, all of these resources can be used in a valid argument for the need to incorporate global skills across the curriculum and in all parts of a school and district. When creating a new learning space, these authors and initiatives can help to reassure a questioning public about the necessity of adaptation, trying new teaching methods, and designing space differently. When parents raise concerns that this mindset is a new type of experiment involving their children, we can confidently answer that the implementation of global skills has moved well beyond the discussion stage and into the realm of best practices, and the design of a new learning space is the next step in the education evolution.

GRADUATE PROFILES

Many schools that have established their own lists of skills have sometimes combined them into a graduate profile that can be used to describe the overall skill set they would like for their students to have upon graduating from their school or district. These profiles, if developed correctly and in conjunction with other 21st century professional development initiatives, can serve as powerful catalysts for change and as the foundation for decision making in multiple areas such as curriculum alignment, professional development, and budgeting. They are a concise way of saying, "Here is a description of what we want to accomplish practically and philosophically."

To form an effective graduate profile, follow these guidelines:

- The document should be brief.

- The document should use vocabulary that is easily understood.

- The document should be thought of as a "working document," meaning it is open to constant examination and adjustment.

- The document should have input from multiple parties if it is to be used on a broad scale and should be reviewed by those who are using it prior to its full implementation.

- The document should reflect both the philosophy of the originators and the best practices of 21st century teaching and learning.

- The document's effectiveness should be assessed in various ways.

- The document should have an official review after a set period of time to ask what worked in the document, what could be better, and what has changed in our district or the world since the document's inception.

One of the first districts to successfully implement a graduate profile was the Leander Independent School District, a large suburban district near Austin, Texas. The profile was first written in the 1990s as the district leadership recognized the changes beginning to transform society with the approach of the digital age. The assistant superintendent for curriculum, Monta Akin, played an instrumental role in its initial conception and subsequent iterations.

To begin the process of forming a profile, Akin asked the essential question of the purpose of educators.

"Why are we here? We are here to learn and have fun."

Those were the first words I heard W. Edwards Deming speak when I had the privilege of attending his seminar for educators in 1992. W. Edwards Deming, an expert in the field of quality, was 92 at the time and had turned his attention to education in his last few years of life.

"A system must have an aim. Without an aim, there is no system," Deming asserted.

(Continued)

(Continued)

Those words from Deming started the wheels turning in my mind. He also was emphatic that it is leadership's responsibility to orchestrate the efforts of all components of the system toward achievement of the stated aim. So, where was I to start?

What are schools for? Indeed, why are we here?

It is no accident that Leander ISD's improvement journey began with a question. Questions guide discussions, and those conversations define a culture. By changing the questions we asked, we changed—and improved—the professional dialogue coursing through our system. As a result, we built a new culture.

- Who is to blame? changed to What do we need to improve? How can we do better?

- What is the problem? changed to How do we know? What evidence do we have to guide our decisions?

- What do we need to do? changed to Who needs to be involved in making this decision?

These questions we began asking were key to making our cultural transformation.

Our questioning to determine the aim of our system led to extended discussions and initiated the lengthy process of developing Leander ISD's Graduate Profile. The document was named the Graduate Profile from the beginning of the process to establish intent:

- Our intent was to develop a document that clarified the expectations of our system.

- Our intent was to develop a document that would be useful throughout the system.

- Our intent was to articulate a promise to our students of what they could expect from their education.

Using an iterative process of gathering and analyzing input from multiple stakeholder groups including staff, students, and community, we distilled the critical attributes. The Leander ISD Graduate Profile became the first of several mutually agreed upon Guiding Documents that provided the foundation for the culture we were seeking to create. Culture has to be actively and thoughtfully created, then continually nurtured. No matter how much you would like to speed up the cultural shift, the reality is you create culture slowly and subtly over a period of time. It cannot be mandated and it cannot be rushed. "(M. Akin, personal communication, April 29, 2015)

THREE STAGES OF DEVELOPMENT

An effective creation of a new type of learning space does not occur in the first stage of an organization's development. As Akin points out, there must first be a culture of trust and then one of continuous improvement before making a shift in thinking. The creation of a new type of learning space can be the third part of this progression.

Leander ISD Graduate Profile

Here is the current Leander ISD graduate profile, used with permission.

Leander ISD students are well prepared to enrich our world and excel in a global society. Each student is challenged, encouraged, and supported to achieve the highest level of knowledge, skills, and character.

Academics

Students are academically prepared for college, career, and life and equipped to achieve their highest potential. Students demonstrate:

Knowledge, understanding, and application of

- *English and language arts*
- *Mathematics*
- *Science*
- *Social studies*
- *U.S. constitutional studies*
- *A second language*

Character Development

Students understand the importance of positive interactions with others as a foundation for living successful lives. Students personify the 10 Ethical Principles:

- *Honesty: telling the truth*
- *Integrity: doing the right thing even when no one is looking*
- *Promise keeping: doing what you say you are going to do*
- *Loyalty: supporting someone or something*
- *Concern for others: caring for and helping others*

- *Law abidance/civic duty: obeying rules and laws; making the world a better place*
- *Respect for others: being polite and kind to everyone and everything*
- *Fairness: treating everyone equally*
- *Pursuit of excellence: doing everything the best you can; looking for ways to improve*
- *Accountability: taking responsibility for your actions and taking pride in what you do right*

Communication

Students communicate and collaborate effectively. Students demonstrate:

- *Proficiency in written communication*
- *Proficiency in oral communication, individually and in groups, including speaking, active listening, and constructive dialogue*
- *Proficiency in preparing and delivering presentations*
- *Ability to work collaboratively as a team*
- *Adaptability and flexibility in response to the audience and environment*
- *Effective use of current technology*

Effective, Productive, and Lifelong Learning

Students possess the aptitude, attitude, and skills necessary for the continuous pursuit of knowledge throughout life. Students demonstrate:

- *Problem-solving skills*
- *Creative and critical-thinking skills*
- *Proficiency in accessing, managing, and processing information*
- *Competency using various learning tools, techniques, and technologies*
- *Perseverance, resiliency, and self-discipline to successfully set goals, develop action plans, manage time, monitor progress, and evaluate results*
- *Ability to learn through collaboration*
- *Ability to reflect and use feedback to continuously improve*
- *Discerning research skills*

Personal Growth and Expression

Students apply their unique talents for personal growth and fulfillment. Students demonstrate:

- *Passion for and ownership of learning*
- *Self-awareness of skills, interests, aptitudes, and learning styles*
- *Personal development and expression through artistic, physical, and intellectual disciplines*
- *Proactive physical wellness*
- *Understanding of fiscal responsibility*
- *Awareness of life opportunities in college and career guidance*

Social Awareness, Contribution, and Stewardship

Students are active contributors in the community and prepared to participate in our global society. Students demonstrate:

- *Contribution and service to community*
- *Stewardship of resources*
- *Understanding the benefits of a democratic government, free enterprise, and entrepreneurship*
- *Leadership skills*
- *Understanding the value of cultural diversity*

The Leander ISD profile, like others, stresses certain skill sets that are important to the school and community for academic, cultural, and political reasons. The extent to which the profile documents these areas and the exact domains and skills presented will vary from school to school. No two profiles are exactly alike—for a graduate profile to have a deep impact on learning and the school's culture, it must reflect both the personality of the school in its current state of development and guide the school in the direction it wishes to go. The outline of the graduate profile, any photos that might accompany it, and any other unique elements allow the designers to be both creative and practical.

Another example of a graduate profile (used here with permission) may be found in the Gahanna-Jefferson Public Schools (Ohio), the home of Clark Hall. The document played a key role in freeing teachers to focus on skills and to search for creative ways to use the learning spaces.

Gahanna-Jefferson Public Schools Graduate Profile

We educate our students to be serious about learning and to thrive in the 21st century global community. Our students will be:

A Responsible Community Member

I can demonstrate a strong work ethic.

I can respect myself, others, and the environment.

I can appreciate the differences in others.

I can model positive character traits and set goals.

I can serve my community and help others.

I can make safe and healthy choices.

A Comprehensive Problem Solver

I can think creatively on my own.

I can find people or resources to help me.

I can develop a plan for different situations.

I can check my plan, decide what to do next, and keep working toward my goal.

A Collaborative Team Member

I can work with others and lead when needed.

I can respect others' ideas, even if they are different from my own.

I can learn from others.

I can be passionate about my beliefs.

An Effective Communicator

I can be a focused and respectful listener.

I can be a quality writer.

I can speak to different audiences.

I can gather and understand information.

I can post, text, tweet, blog, and comment responsibly when using social media.

A Skillful Technology User

I can choose technology and information that will help me achieve my goals.

I can creatively use different technology to show what I have learned.

I can use technology to share information as I work with others.

I can use technology responsibly and honestly.

Our Commitment

Each student will receive a rigorous academic foundation in English, mathematics, science, social studies, economics, foreign language, fine arts, speech technology applications, physical and health educations, and optional courses. Each student will be able to pursue educational opportunities relevant to individual interests. The relationships the student develops with peers, staff, and community members throughout the journey will support the transformation from student to educated, responsible citizen.

Process for Creating a Graduate Profile

The collaborative process used in Gahanna is similar to the one used in Leander, and it can be used as one way of forming a list of global skills into a graduate profile. The original version of this document was written as the district's educators began their shift to a model of thinking that empowered students, incorporated global skills, and began to rely more heavily on technology.

To create the first document, a group of administrators, teachers, and high school students met monthly during one school year. They debated the skills they wished to incorporate, the format, and the overall philosophy they wished to convey through the profile. It was seen as both a statement of who they were as a district and as a working document that could be used to guide them in their decision making.

A critical point made by the committee, as was the case in Leander, is that this document was *not* just a high school document. Whereas it would depict the overall picture of the qualities an accomplished district graduate should possess, it also represented the goals that should be prevalent in all classrooms from the kindergarten level to the senior year. A district's graduate is educated in all parts of the district, not just the high school; thus, this document was K–12 in its vision.

In studying other graduate profiles from around America it found online, the committee liked the ones that had pictures of those districts' students at the top of the profile, as if the picture stood as a solid reminder that this document was a student-centered piece. Bright colors could be used—preferably school colors—for this document that would be placed throughout the community, and it could be reproduced in various sizes from 8" x 11" fliers to large posters.

When the profile was released for use throughout the district, posters were placed in most classrooms and in prominent places in offices and hallways for students, educators, and visitors to constantly view. The document was widely accepted for three reasons.

1. It represented the next step in the district's mind shift that had begun with book studies; with discussions of global skills and 21st century students; and with professional development that focused on technology usage, the role of grades in student assessment, and other best practices.

2. There was broad representation and ownership because the document's composers represented all levels of teaching and administration and all buildings in the district. The student perspective was represented through the inclusion of the district's high school students, and the members were getting constant feedback during the writing process and sharing information at critical points in its development.

3. It was a one-page document that was easy to read and understand. The committee felt that the document should be user-friendly and not be filled with educational terminology or any sort of stilted language; it needed to be written so that students could understand it.

The profile affected the district culture in a positive manner. Some schools developed Graduate Profile Awards for students who did exemplary jobs of exhibiting the skills, and the names or pictures of students who excelled in these skills were sometimes posted on bulletin boards. At the high school, a Graduate Profile Scholarship was established and funded by the principal and teachers. An important point to note about these awards is that they were not always given to the top academic students—these skills could be exhibited by all students, including those who might be struggling academically but were allowed to shine in areas not normally recognized in classrooms. At the district office level, questions asked about new initiatives or purchasing might be, "How does this initiative fit our graduate profile?" and "Is this expenditure going to advance the skills and philosophy of our graduate profile?"

After three years, the committee reconvened, with some new members to offer fresh ideas, and it revisited the document and made adjustments based on its research of the latest trends of 21st century learning and the feedback it had received from district members about the first version. A key change was made based on the feedback from the elementary teachers:

when the first version had been released some of the elementary teachers rewrote it in "I Can" statements, which made it much easier for the elementary students to comprehend and to apply. The "I Can" version made its way into middle school and high school classrooms, and this edition was more popular than the original document, which had been written in traditional third-person style. Thus, the recommendation from teachers of all levels was that the updated version of the graduate profile be written as "I Can" statements.

BREAKING DOWN A GRADUATE PROFILE INTO SEGMENTS

It is essential to note that the process used by the Gahanna-Jefferson Public Schools is just one way of developing a graduate profile. There are numerous ways to write a profile, and different segments and skill sets can be placed in different sequences.

For example, in the Gahanna-Jefferson Public Schools' graduate profile, the first segment is the introduction, which is a broad statement from the profile's creators to show the district wishes to educate its students in a 21st century manner.

> *We educate our students to be serious about learning and to thrive in the 21st century global community.*

One of the most important elements of the district's culture was the strong tie between the community and its public schools, so the first skill set to be presented covered the skills needed to be a responsible community member. The community prided itself on its work ethic, its diversity, its positive reputation, and its long history of promoting service, and those skills are prominently displayed. The committee discussed the importance of nurturing the entire student and of teaching young people to make healthy decisions for the rest of their lives.

A Responsible Community Member

> *I can demonstrate a strong work ethic.*
>
> *I can respect myself, others, and the environment.*
>
> *I can appreciate the differences in others.*
>
> *I can model positive character traits and set goals.*
>
> *I can serve my community and help others.*
>
> *I can make safe and healthy choices.*

The next skill set chosen was that of critical thinking. The committee felt it was important to present this set early so that it could let the reader know of the importance of critical thinking and creativity in the 21st century and to let it balance with the previous skill set of service. The last skill of checking the plan and being an assertive problem solver was a desire to instill in students a sense of grit, to help them understand that achieving greatness often takes extreme effort.

A Comprehensive Problem Solver

I can think creatively on my own.

I can find people or resources to help me.

I can develop a plan for different situations.

I can check my plan, decide what to do next, and keep working toward my goal.

In the next skill set, the domain of collaboration was presented. Notice these skills promote a combination of leadership, cooperation, learning, and an element that is not quite a skill but is just as critical when exploring creativity and entrepreneurship: passion.

A Collaborative Team Member

I can work with others and lead when needed.

I can respect others' ideas, even if they are different from my own.

I can learn from others.

I can be passionate about my beliefs.

In the communicator skill set, the committee stressed the importance of listening, writing, speaking, and gathering information. The final skill, posting on social media with responsibility, was added to help deal with an issue common everywhere: of young people sometimes posting inappropriate messages or photos online.

An Effective Communicator

I can be a focused and respectful listener.

I can be a quality writer.

I can speak to different audiences.

I can gather and understand information.

I can post, text, tweet, blog, and comment responsibly when using social media.

Though technology was listed as the final skill set, it was not last because it was deemed least important. On the contrary, the committee felt the technology skills could be seen as both the foundation of 21st century learning and the area where all of the skills culminated: with students using technology to help others, to solve problems, to collaborate, and to communicate.

A Skillful Technology User

> *I can choose technology and information that will help me achieve my goals.*
>
> *I can creatively use different technology to show what I have learned.*
>
> *I can use technology to share information as I work with others.*
>
> *I can use technology responsibly and honestly.*

In this profile all academic subjects are listed in a special section at the end of the document as a reminder that the district is still committed to academics. The committee listed more than the traditional subjects; it wanted all fields represented, including the fine arts and physical and health education. To conclude the document, the final two sentences summarize the philosophy of the district: that all students should be allowed to pursue individual interests, and the district recognized the importance of relationships in the transformative journey to "educated, responsible citizen."

Our Commitment

Each student will receive a rigorous academic foundation in English, mathematics, science, social studies, economics, foreign language, fine arts, speech technology applications, physical and health educations, and optional courses. Each student will be able to pursue educational opportunities relevant to individual interests. The relationships the student develops with peers, staff, and community members throughout the journey will support the transformation from student to educated, responsible citizen.

GLOBAL SKILLS AT RIVER BLUFF HIGH SCHOOL

Again, there is no right or wrong way to create a graduate profile: each document is a reflection of the philosophies, attitudes, personalities, histories, and vision of the different districts. The beauty of creating these documents is that each district can craft versions that are unique and stand as symbols for that district.

Another school that has used a graduate profile of global skills to guide its construction and educational programming is River Bluff High School, in Lexington, South Carolina. Under the leadership of Dr. Karen Woodward, Lexington County School District One has created a document that prompts students to be "self-directed, creative, collaborative, caring, and multilingual."

Guidance for global skills in South Carolina is also coming from the state level. The state of South Carolina has a list of skills authored by the South Carolina Chamber of Commerce and the South Carolina Association of School Administrators Superintendent's Round Table that promotes a global perspective for all of its graduates. The domains are designed to promote world-class knowledge, life and career characteristics, and world-class skills.

When the district needed to build a new, large high school, Dr. Woodward and the school's principal, Dr. Luke Clamp, decided to build a different type of high school centered on 21st century learners. Today, River Bluff High School combines innovative scheduling, global skills, student-held technology, and innovative learning space to educate its students. Dr. Clamp describes their high school:

Profile (Student Outcomes) for 21st Century Graduates

Self Directed, creative, collaborative, caring and multilingual

Confident in academics
World class knowledge (SC)
21st century content (liberal arts, 3R's, STEM, multiple languages) (SC)
College, Career and Citizenship Ready (SC)

Sophisticated in learning
Self-directed - applies learning independently to solve problems, initiates and plans course of action, self monitors and self corrects. (SC)
Knows how to learn (SC)
Acquires and applies information and technology for analysis and research
Creates innovative solutions (SC)

Accomplished in 21st century skills
4 C's: Critical thinking, Collaboration, Creativity, Communication (SC)
Digital/media fluency (SC)
Life and Career Skills (SC)

Global in orientation (SC)
Knowledgeable about global issues and interconnectedness
Understands cultures and demonstrates sensitivity to differentness
Multilingual

Prepared as a leader and global citizen
Understands responsibilities of citizenship and capable leadership
Ethical and caring
Understanding of civic literacy
Possession of leadership habits, skills and attitude, life and career skills

▶ River Bluff High School

River Bluff High School, a comprehensive public high school serving grades 9–12 . . . models how to create a personalized learning environment for every student. It embraces technology and is rooted in a design to challenge every student to engage in ownership of their own learning. . . . Referenced in the profile of the 21st century graduate, students at River Bluff have the expectation of graduating sophisticated in learning and global in orientation accomplished in 21st century learning skills and prepared as leaders and global citizens. . . . The history is important to connect to the story of River Bluff High School, as it was designed to meet the needs of a 21st century graduate, not fitting the students into the design of a school. The layout also supports professional collaboration and inquiry as teachers are not confined to four walled classrooms, isolated from their peers, but are provided large collaborative common areas with individual open-air work stations with adjacent work areas for students to invite both teacher and peer interaction at a moment's notice.

Providing comfortable, flexible spaces for students to engage with their work is another key feature to the design of River Bluff as it is home to four two-story collaborative common areas that combine teacher work stations with student collaborative space. Each department is housed in a commons area, and they connect each of the four wings together. These spaces are alive as students engage with their work independently or collaboratively and provide access to their teachers in a friendly and safe environment. Teachers have reported that while they were anxious about giving up their room that they were home to for years, they are not sure how they would ever go back to an environment that was not so visibly collaborative. For students who seek a quieter space for learning and research, they may choose the Learning Commons, which is located in the center of campus. The learning spaces are full of natural light, and soft airy tones were selected to invoke a calm environment for learning. The feedback from students has been that River Bluff feels like home.

Furniture selection was key as the word flexible continued to emerge in the research. Trips to Steelcase in Grand Rapids, Michigan, provided firsthand experience in seeing new designs for educational furniture. In the classroom spaces, rectangular and semicircular tables were selected along with movable chairs to allow for the instructional environment to shift and move into the setting most conducive for the instructional delivery. It is common to see the setting transform into two circles for a Socratic seminar and then transition into collaborative groups and end in a lecture setting for wrap-up activities. Also in the corridor areas and large common areas, soft couches,

(Continued)

(Continued)

ottomans, and chairs were selected to provide a safe environment that felt like home. Technology infrastructure was key as a wireless overlay envelops the entire campus and each classroom is equipped with a 70 inch flat-screen TV and an Apple TV wireless device for projection. Each student is provided a one-to-one mobile computing device—an iPad 2 Air—and teachers engage their instruction digitally through a learning management system called Schoology. This platform is used for enrichment, support in digital assessment and planning of instruction, communicating current content to students, and communicating academic data to both students and parents. (L. Clamp, personal communication, June 30, 2015)

▶ River Bluff High School

Clamp and his staff keep students at the center of instruction. He says the students at River Bluff High School don't need bells to guide them to class and that they can control significant parts of their learning. Here is how he describes the beginning of a typical day.

The 8:15 a.m. bell begins to welcome students into their first module (mod) class. Students enter calmly remembering that the only other bell they will hear is the bell at 3:40 p.m. ending the school day.

Independent Learning Time (ILT) became the vehicle on campus for students to take ownership of their learning and engage with both peers and teachers. The schedule consists of 15 modes of time that are 30 minutes in length in a 5 day cycle that repeats each week for 36 weeks. Courses are grouped in time groups of 30, 60, or 90 minutes a day and could meet three or four days a week within two different phases. Courses are taught in small groups (20–25 students) two or three times a week, and some are taught in large groups (50–90 students) once a week. Only a bell to begin and end school interrupts the school day as students manage their time digitally and transition from space to space efficiently.

Expected to engage, create, discuss, and defend, students at River Bluff High School . . . own the expectation to be leaders of their own learning. . . . The design for River Bluff began with the student in mind, a backward design process beginning with the end in mind. Students and teachers are thinking in a new direction. . . . Designing and using the learning space differently began with the who—not just the persons who would occupy the space for employment, but the persons who would occupy the space for learning—the students. (L. Clamp, personal communication, June 30, 2015)

▶ River Bluff High School

The design, function, and programming were so important to the district that Dr. Clamp was appointed two years prior to the school opening. Dr. Luke and the district took a different approach in hiring his 21st century staff, and the school's future students, parents, and community members helped with the planning.

> The identification of these certified positions began with professional criteria, not certifications. A year before the school opened, the students who were geographically zoned to attend all had decision-making power, selecting the school's mascot and color scheme and developing the alma mater and a few traditions. Engagement with the community in vision visits—community open houses—early on in the process allowed for school leaders to meet families and community members in neighborhood clubhouses and church fellowship halls to discuss the new vision for learning and how the instructional and facility design was created strategically for all the "who" that would occupy River Bluff. (L. Clamp, personal communication, June 30, 2015)

▶ River Bluff High School

MEDIA CENTER REDESIGNS

One of the first groups of educators to redesign its learning space to fit the needs of Generation Z and their need for global skills has been the media center specialists at the K–12 level. The media centers, or libraries, have always been places where students gather to do research or to read and work on papers and projects. Some of the specialists who run these centers saw the students evolving—and they took steps to ensure their spaces fit the needs of this new type of student.

As Gahanna Lincoln High School was going through its redesign process for Clark Hall and other areas in its school, media specialist Ann Gleek was quick to spot the potential for her library.

As a high school librarian at a school that is over 100 years old, I used to spend a lot of time dreaming about renovating my library. I suffered from a severe case of "library envy" any time I walked into a new school building and saw huge windows, new furniture, and circulation desks. It was my dream to have a library space that students wanted to utilize. I wanted students to have a comfortable environment and actually enjoy spending time in the library, not a space where students came to grab a book and quickly leave. It always took a little air out of my sails when I went back to my library where we had outdated furniture from the early 1960s, a small square room, and no windows. Then one day my principal stopped by and asked me if I would like to reinvent my library space. Immediately, I jumped at this idea. My brain started fantasizing about furniture catalogs and contacting architects to write up plans for my new library. Quickly, I had to come back to reality as my principal informed me that there would be little to no extra money available to make this renovation happen. How could I change my space with no funding? This is when I had to start thinking of ways that I could make small changes with a large impact.

My first priority was to reevaluate my current budget. I knew that if I wanted to reinvent my space, I would have to spend money. Since I wasn't going to get any additional resources, I had to look at my budget and determine what revisions I could make. Ultimately, I found that I could spend less in books and supplies for a year in order to make changes to the space. I could easily justify spending less in those areas because if I provided students with a setting that made them comfortable, then my circulation would increase—with or without the newest materials.

Once I figured out where to find the money, I had to figure out how to transform the space on a very limited budget. The first thing I wanted to do was create more space. In order to do this, I spent a great deal of time weeding out old materials from my collection so that I could get rid of old shelving units that blocked light and cluttered the space. Upon removal, the room completely opened up. Now that I have an open floor plan, the room seems larger and there is a better overall atmosphere in the room. The best thing about this change was that it didn't cost anything.

Next, I proceeded to use the small budget I had reallocated. I started by painting the walls. The room was taupe, like the rest of the school building. I wanted a change, so I went bold. I painted the walls white and painted accent

(Continued)

(Continued)

walls in bright, bold colors—neon green, orange, and bright blue. The impact of a little paint was amazing. The library immediately transformed into a more comfortable and welcoming place for the students. I then purchased small sets of modern, comfortable furniture. (I have been purchasing a few pieces a year since the first year.) Having small areas with couches encouraged students to relax and read, collaborate with other students, or simply hang out before or after school. The comfortable furniture became very popular, and I saw my student library usage increase rapidly.

Honestly, the hardest part of the renovation was getting it out of my head. I would often consult with my principal and repeatedly question my new ideas. I worried that my plans wouldn't work or that it wasn't in the best interest of the students. In the end, I found that the only thing holding me back was my fear of change since it had always been the other way for so long. Once I reinvented the library space, I knew I had made the correct decision. I was able to actualize a space that students use and love. In fact, my daily library visits from students went from 92 students a day to over 150 students each day. More students visiting the space also meant more circulation of books, more use of computers and technology, and more time for me to assist students and teach information literacy skills. (A. Gleek, personal communication, February 26, 2015)

The GLHS library before the space redesign effort.

▶ Ann Gleek

WHAT'S IN YOUR SPACE?

▶ Ann Gleek

▶ Ann Gleek

The GLHS library after the space redesign.

▶ Ann Gleek

A space redesign can also be popular with middle school students. Karie Gregory is the librarian of Middle School West in Gahanna. She, too, looked at her traditional library and knew she wanted to improve it.

Five years ago I became the library/media specialist at my 6–8 building. The library's appearance was not very kid-friendly. Beige walls. Standard library tables. So my two administrators wanted me to (in their words) "drop a bomb on the place." I had free reign and administrative blessing to redesign the entire library.

My goal was to design a space that welcomed students. I wanted them to want to hang out here. I knew I couldn't do everything I had in mind in the four weeks I had before school started—I wouldn't have the time or the budget. I started with creating a couple of comfy seating areas—loveseats, crazy carpet, chairs, lamps, etc. It required budget reallocations; I had to sacrifice purchasing some books in order to buy the furniture. However, I started heavily weeding tired old books out of the collection. This made the shelves look bright and attractive, and suddenly the newer titles were more noticeable and accessible. Fewer books also meant more room to display books face-out on the shelves. This (along with moving the books and shelves around for better flow) was all that I accomplished that first August before school started, but it made a huge impact. Students felt like they were coming back to a new library.

Next, I worked on getting rid of the beige walls. Some colors (the neon green, for example) were student choices. I put the paint wheel in front of groups of kids in the library and asked them to pick their favorites. Because the walls were due to be repainted that year anyway (the same boring beige), the custodial staff took care of repainting over breaks and weekends that first year.

▶ Karie Gregory

(Continued)

(Continued)

Fortunately, the library was also due for some new tables to replace a few broken ones. Instead of replacing them with more of the same, I asked for four high-top tables and tall stools, which immediately became student favorites. Over the next few years, I added a little of this and a little of that. The PTO at my building was kind enough to purchase a "restaurant booth" for the library, which has been a big hit with the students. It's the first place they head. A rocking chair and ficus tree here, a few more bean bags there, and before I knew it just about every bit of usable space was devoted to comfy seating for reading and working.

▶ Karie Gregory

In addition to creating comfortable seating for independent reading and work, I also created a couple of small-group workspaces. I gutted the Reference Room, getting rid of the outdated encyclopedias. Then I turned the Reference Room into an area for small-group work and/or audiobook listening. I turned my library office into another meeting room. I moved in 2 large tables and 10 chairs and reorganized all of my own library materials. It's used constantly by teachers and students for meetings, group work, etc. I have more requests to use those two small-group work areas than I ever would have dreamed. Students meeting in groups also frequently use the restaurant booth.

▶ Karie Gregory

In addition to making the appearance of the library more kid-friendly and adding more small-group meeting spaces, I made some other changes to bring more students in and facilitate book circulation. When I first got the job, the fiction books were all the way in the back of the library, behind a large bank of computers. The nonfiction books were closer to the door, right near all the new comfy seating. This was completely counterproductive. So I "hired" my husband and three sons, and together we moved over 8,000 books, totally swapping the locations of the fiction and the nonfiction sections in the four weeks before school started. Now, the fiction books are in shorter, easily browsed shelves, with plenty of top surfaces for displaying new and featured titles. They are also conveniently located near the seating areas. The nonfiction section is now behind the computers. There is a logical division between pleasure reading areas and research/information areas. I also began adding manga and graphic novels. I will defend the literary worth of graphic novels to the moon and back, and having a strong graphic novel/manga selection brings in a whole new clientele of kids who otherwise would never voluntarily set foot in a library.

I also needed to make some changes regarding technology in the library. The bank of 15 desktop computers was not sufficient for even one typical

(Continued)

(Continued)

class's needs. So, through grants, more budget reallocation, begging for some building funds, and even a donation or two, I gradually acquired iPads, Chromebooks, and a few laptops for more flexible technology use, both in location and in function. iPads are ideal for some things, but not for others. Same with Chromebooks.

If I could give other educators advice on redesigning their learning spaces, I would tell them to first think about function over appearance. It's not redecorating, it's redesigning. Why do you want to change up your space? What is it you want students to do in the space? Look for the free changes you can make (such as rearranging furniture). Also, don't waste time looking up pictures of other people's learning spaces or stalking Pinterest boards. You don't want to copy someone else's space, because they won't have the exact same needs or resources you do. It will limit your own creativity, and it could lead to envy and frustration. Also, talk to the students. Some of my best ideas came from student suggestions. Finally, don't try to do everything at once. Let your space evolve little by little based on your own needs and resources. My greatest challenges were— and continue to be—time, space, and money. I could do such great things with more of all three!

One thing I've noticed since redoing the library and throwing the doors wide open is that teachers and students are craving just plain project and group workspace. Whether it's student small groups, teacher-and-student small groups and one-on-one, or individual/independent work, students and teachers need flexible workspaces dedicated for those purposes. I am really trying to turn the library into a learning center or a work center rather than just a place to get great books (although I pride myself on that as well). My future goals include finding a way to create more project workspaces, for both media and traditional formats.

It's too bad more of those kinds of spaces aren't designed into our school buildings. And extra spaces like that could be flexible, as well. Having a guest speaker? Need extra space for state-mandated testing? Your students need to spread out and paint shower curtains as part of a project? Your students need to work in small groups using iPads to capture video? Flexible work and learning spaces would serve all of those needs. Unfortunately, in schools we tend to use every square inch of our buildings in very inflexible ways. (K. Gregory, personal communication, May 12, 2015)

Z SPACES AT THE ELEMENTARY LEVEL

Elementary teachers have often been at the forefront of designing their learning space around their learners, and some elementary teachers today continue to evaluate their use of classroom space. Erin Klein is an award-winning second grade teacher who was Michigan's Teacher of the Year in 2014. When she redesigned her learning space she began by viewing her classroom through different eyes—the eyes of her students.

When I thought about my own classroom space, I went to sit in one of my student's desks. Though I'm larger than the average second-grader, it was soon easy for me to realize how the furniture and layout did not lend itself for collaboration and comfort. I wanted my students to gather on the carpet, sit in nooks, and work with one another. I had a vision of children using the space freely, as needed, to do meaningful work with one another. However, I had not given them a proper space to facilitate these sorts of activities. Instead, the oversized, cold, hard desks were taking over every square foot of my room. This furniture was chunky. Even though I had the desks in groups to encourage discussion, they were still so far from one another just due to the sheer size of the tabletops. When children tried to turn eye-to-eye and knee-to-knee to work with a partner, the massive, steel desk compartments separated them. Why can't my classroom look like a creative play space in a museum or the children's section of a Barnes and Noble?

The more I thought about why my classroom couldn't resemble a space like that in a museum or a bookstore, I began to realize that in order for this to happen, I had to be the change that sparked this idea into motion. Instead of wishing I had a classroom space that my students would flourish in and appreciate, I had to design it, find funding, and get ideas from the clients (my kids!). How often are students asked how they would like their classroom set up? After all, who are the ones who will be using this space the most?

When I asked my students how we should think about setting up our classroom for the new year, many of them expressed the importance of having areas where they could sit and relax. They really enjoyed being able to stretch out with a good book and not be confined to their desk. That's when I began brainstorming creative ways to incorporate inviting seating areas that would help to maximize the layout's working area. We "ditched the desks" in second grade to provide a more functional learning landscape.

(Continued)

(Continued)

Since we have a small room, it was essential to utilize each section of the space. Our corner breakfast nook works perfectly to provide additional seating since it tucks right into the corner, not taking up unnecessary floor space. The bench seats also lift to provide extra storage. I keep many of our charging cords and technology accessories in these cubbies.

▶ Erin Klein

We use this area for groups to collaborate together and work on projects with one another. There are also two round tables in the center of the room for children to use while working independently or with partners. We have 20 iPads for our grade level this year, which will be shared among four classes. So I am excited to have a comfortable area for children to connect with each other as they develop content and extend lessons on the iPads.

Having studied interior design prior to going into teaching, I knew there would be a few key elements that would be instrumental in this redesign process. Along with creating flexible seating arrangements, it was imperative to declutter the space and minimize the environmental print. This was to be a true student-centered space. If I had materials that had not been used within the past year or two, it was time to remove them from the space. I also ensured that all materials and resources were at the children's eye level and reach. Removing laminate also helped to make sure there wasn't a glare on anything that was posted for students. During the school day, we minimize the use of overhead fluorescent lighting and utilize natural lighting and incandescent lighting via lamps placed around the room. Another key element was to reduce the variety of colors and patterns displayed around the room that could be distracting for some learners. We selected a monochromatic color palate that was warm and inviting. One last simple change we made was to bring in nature to add a touch of green to the space and allow children the opportunity to care for the plants. These simple redesign changes allow us to have a classroom learning environment that fosters comfort, creativity, and collaboration. (E. Klein, personal communication, May 3, 2015)

INDIVIDUAL-TEACHER OR SMALL-TEAM SKILL LISTS

Though there is power to effect institutional change through these district-implemented graduate profiles, they do not have to be administratively driven; if a district does not have a list of global skills, then individual teachers or small teams of teachers can commit to researching the topic and forming their own list of skills.

Some teachers might be advancing in their growth beyond that of the school in which the teachers work. Individual teachers or small groups of teachers can work the skills into their classrooms without disrupting the set curriculum. In many classrooms, especially those using a curriculum that is somewhat skills based, such as the CCSS, these expanded lists could enhance the accepted curriculum and allow the teacher to delve more deeply into an area in which much of the world is heading.

For example, a high school English teacher could research the educational websites that promote global skills, study the graduate profiles used in various other schools, examine the skills in his or her own curriculum, and then begin to form a list of skills under the domains of communication, creativity, critical thinking, and collaboration. These are skills covered in almost any language arts class, but forming such a list could help the teacher to focus even more sharply on what is being accomplished and to adjust the curriculum and assessment accordingly.

A high school math department could decide that it would like to focus on one of the skills, such as communication, and it could research the different ways students should be able to communicate today. It could then rework some of its lessons to promote more group work and more individual and group presentations.

A seventh-grade social studies team could dedicate its efforts to communication and collaboration, and it could use one of the global education sites that links classrooms from around the world to do a joint project with a school on another continent. It could promote Skyping, research, and a greater social understanding, which are other global skills in which the students would be immersed.

Some of the greatest teaching of 21st century skills is found in elective classrooms such as art, drama, choir, band, and orchestra. In all of these classrooms, students must create, work together, present their work, and think critically of the product they are displaying. In this era of budget cuts, the arts should be the last group to be reduced. As teachers of the arts promote their courses, they should do more than say their subjects spring from the heart. They should also be stressing that the arts classes are some of the greatest classrooms in the world for promoting creativity and global skills. The arts promote an entrepreneurial way of thinking that allows students to apply their knowledge gained in the core subjects, and they help to develop people who can view the entire world through a creative lens.

Of course, teachers at the elementary level could play huge roles in developing 21st century skills in young people. Collaboration and communication have always been significant components of elementary schooling, and teachers at that level have stressed civic responsibility, ethics, creativity, and critical thinking. Creating a 21st century skill set would allow the teachers to hone their curriculum and assess their students from a new perspective. Not only are they teaching students to effectively share a classroom space, but they are also giving them the skills they will need to navigate the twists and turns of the 21st century.

Even a kindergarten class could realize its part in the skills paradigm. The teaching of basic skills begins in these primary classrooms, and kindergarten teachers do more than present the first strands of information to their students. They are already preparing students for life 50 years into the future in a time when we can only imagine how the world will look and the types of jobs they will have. What kind of skills should kindergarten teachers be teaching today? Besides providing coping skills and an academic foundation, kindergarten teachers must teach the 4 C's, and like other teachers they should do it in a systematic way that allows for student freedom, varied assessments, and a reflection by the teacher on the progress made and the next steps to be taken.

Clearly, there is a capability for teachers at all levels to incorporate global skills into their curriculum. If the initiative is not district driven, then it can be individually driven.

PROFESSIONAL DEVELOPMENT
IDEAS TO TEACH GLOBAL SKILLS
Collaborate

- Work with other educators to determine if you will create a full graduate profile of global skills or begin with a simple outline.

- Form a group of teachers in your subject or at your grade level and analyze an updated version of Bloom's taxonomy. List lessons, teaching practices, or assessment models that correspond with each skill level.

- Have a discussion with teachers in other grade levels or subjects and determine which skills they stress and compare them with yours. Also, form a list of the skills not being stressed so you can begin to implement them.

- Work with teachers, coaches, and club sponsors to examine the global skills taught in the arts, physical education, and extracurricular activities. Publicize the list for the community to see.

- Discuss global skills with your students and ask them how you can work with them to make the curriculum, instruction, and assessment more relevant.

Think Critically

- List the characteristics of two types of classrooms: one dedicated to helping students pass a standardized test and one dedicated to helping students to become fully developed global citizens. Examine their similarities and differences.

- Study the time set aside each year for professional development and based on your needs, allocate a certain percentage of the time to the study and implementation of global skills.

- Think of the projects and assignments for which you teach global skills and begin to imagine how you and your students could use space differently when you teach those lessons.

Create

- Create a vignette that would describe the teaching and learning space to which you wish to transition and write a second vignette describing your current teaching and use of learning space.

- Search for websites that link classrooms from around the world and work with a teacher on another continent to develop a joint project between your classes.

Communicate

- Share the district and school efforts to implement global skills with students, staff, parents, and the community.

- Publicly praise individual schools, teachers, classrooms, and projects that promote global skills.

Stretch to the Future

- Research global skills being stressed in the rest of the world's schools and compare those skills with ones being taught in your school.

- Create a system of continuous improvement in which you will analyze your curriculum periodically to adjust to the changing needs of the students.

Global Skills Research

Study four global skills sources (e.g., websites, books, graduate profiles, standards) and list their similarities and differences.

WHAT IS THE NAME OF THE SOURCE?	WHAT ARE THE MAIN SKILL AREAS EMPHASIZED BY THE SOURCE?	WHAT ARE THE SUBSKILLS LISTED WITHIN THOSE MAIN SKILL AREAS?	WHAT OTHER COMMENTS CAN BE MADE ABOUT THIS SOURCE?
1.			
2.			
3.			
4.			

Curriculum Analysis

Shifting to a global skills–based curriculum means that your curriculum is built on skills—not units, chapters, or textbooks. However, this doesn't mean you should discard all parts of your traditional curriculum. A number of those components could already be built on the skills that have come to the forefront in this century. For example, a number of activities in many classrooms have always emphasized creativity, collaboration, communication, and critical thinking, but they were never examined through a global lens. Examine your current curriculum and find the activities or units that already have a strong global skills component built into their teaching, student activities, or student assessment and search for ways to improve them.

WHAT IS THE UNIT OR ACTIVITY?	WHAT SKILL(S) ARE EXHIBITED IN THE UNIT OR ACTIVITY?	ARE THERE WAYS TO ENHANCE THIS UNIT OR ACTIVITY?
1.		
2.		
3.		
4.		
5.		
6.		
7.		

Create a List of Global Skills

After researching global skills and analyzing the skills already present in your curriculum, make a master list of global skills that will be implemented in the redesigned learning space. Do it in the form of an outline, a full graduate profile, or in some other format that is useful for you.

STEP 5

Let Students Use Technology

Several years ago a group of educators met with a senior computer engineer at the Dell headquarters in Round Rock, Texas. When asked how computers would function 30 years from now, the engineer paused and then answered, "Whatever we think of as magic today will be a daily part of our lives in 30 years" (personal communication with the author, 2010).

Try to imagine what magic might look like in our future learning spaces. Imagine a classroom with a strong network that doesn't crash and where all students have premier devices. The devices might be tablets, computers, or something of which we have not yet dreamed. Try to see a future where apps make words, graphics, and voices jump off of the computer screen.

That magic day is coming. It's only a matter of time. The price of devices and other technology continues to drop as innovations are made, and in the not-so-distant future even schools will have access to top-of-the-line technology. A new era is coming when functioning computers are as common in future classrooms as calculators are in today's classrooms. This will be a gradual shift, and we must take steps now with our practices and our space design to transition into it.

We can dream of a better future, but students today won't wait for that day when all of the computers work. They are sitting in our classrooms now, and this is our one chance to educate them. As we shift to a new type of learning space, we must use the technology we currently have, differentiate our instruction, and let students plug their own computers, tablets, and cell phones into their learning as often as possible.

As you design new and varied types of learning space, be thinking of how students will use technology in the space now and in the future. Will they work alone? In small groups? What kind of presentation spaces will they need when they share their work with teachers and students, and what technology needs to be available in those spaces to provide clear, professional, quality presentations?

The key word will be *flexibility*. We can't see the future, but we know schools and their spaces will function differently.

WE NEED TECHNOLOGY

Today, schools are almost the only places left where students write by hand; when they are away from school they text, type, and FaceTime. So shouldn't the full power of the Internet be at the center of any space redesign? As we make our plans we should recognize that students of almost all ages constantly want to interact with technology and that their future will be filled with technology that is almost unimaginable today. If our schools are truly going to prepare students to thrive in a global economy and to live fully developed lives, then they must implement a strong technology infrastructure on which the devices run, provide more devices for student usage, shift their instruction to include more online components, and design learning spaces that allow students to use technology to work quietly, to create products with small groups of other students, and to have venues where they can present their work and focus on their communication skills.

If we need more proof about where our global society is heading and its impact on education, consider the findings of IBM's big data study that was released in 2012. It revealed some startling truths about technology and our global transformation. In a little over a century, the time in which it took our knowledge to double had dropped from 100 years to 25 years to 13 months. The study told us that an incredible 90 percent of the world's data had been collected in the past two years. Furthermore, the study predicts that as the Internet becomes more developed in the future, knowledge is expected to double every 12 hours (Schilling, 2013).

In other words, we are reaching a point where students will get out of bed at 6:00 in the morning, go to school, and then return home for dinner, and the knowledge created in their world that day while they sat in our schools will have doubled.

And that will happen every day and continue to accelerate.

So, what kind of education should we be providing for these students? How much memorization should students do today in their courses and on assessments when knowledge is growing so rapidly it will be impossible to mentally keep track of it? The information is available at their fingertips via electronic devices. As we design a 21st century learning space, let's discuss the growth of knowledge, global skills, and Generation Z—and how technology can tie them all together.

A teacher who has successfully blended technology and a new type of learning space is Martha Lackey, who teaches third grade in Texas.

> It all started with a district initiative to roll out one-to-one iPads for each of the elementary campuses. Only one teacher per campus was chosen through an application process, and I was selected for my campus. This would

challenge me to redesign my entire classroom for my second- and third-grade bilingual students. I redesigned my entire classroom from furniture to lighting. The process started with a book I read that summer titled *The Third Teacher* (I highly recommend that book). I immediately began thinking about what that was going to look like and began sketching it out on paper. I worked alone as I kept redesigning my classroom. I would pin other classrooms on Pinterest and visit district websites who had a similar vision of what I wanted. (Eanes ISD in Austin and technology leaders had shared their ideas and the process with us.) I brought in lots of lamps and lights and fake trees to create quiet learning spaces when needed. The kids love it when I turn off the lights!

My greatest challenges were getting rid of excess supplies off the floor (book baskets, crates, clunky furniture, etc. to create spaces where students could move freely). This is critical to classroom traffic flow. When I decided to take on this challenge, I asked my principal if I could get rid of all desks and chairs and bring in tables and special types of chairs into my classroom. I received support from all my administrators and my principal gladly said yes. Whatever I needed to do to make learning transformational in my classroom they would support me 100%. So the desks and chairs went out! I brought in round tables and purchased bean bag chairs from Walmart and applied for a DonorsChoose project and received several Hokki stools as well. I also received a picnic table from a parent as a gift for my new classroom design. I created spaces where the students could collaborate freely in a variety of learning spaces and the students adapted quite well. The students rotate to each of the spaces daily throughout the week using the Daily 5 Management System in my classroom.

This kind of learning has transformed me as an educator and has made the learning visible and transformational. The students are more engaged and are able to collaborate freely and work together in groups or partners. I have seen a change in their learning, and the students take more risks in making decisions without my help. They are not afraid to make decisions on their own because they feel safe in this kind of environment. This was my ultimate goal. Taking ownership of their learning and building relationships with each other and me was what I wanted them to achieve, and they have done just that!

My students use their iPads and Chromebooks on a daily basis and move constantly throughout the classroom, which makes their learning come alive. The energy in my classroom is chaotic yet productive. The students love moving around collaborating with other students that may need help with a certain app or project they are working on. This kind of learning works. I have seen it and can say that it will transform the learning in you and your

(Continued)

(Continued)

students. I continue to redesign my classroom each year as I learn from others who are taking the plunge. I would say to those educators who are thinking about this kind of redesigning and teaching that I have never looked back and can't imagine teaching any other way. It's energetic and creates a kind of learning that is the future of how our students will be learning in the next century. They will build relationships with each other that will last a lifetime—it doesn't get any better than that. I have had these students for two years with these devices, and they have learned a lifetime of technology. I am no longer a teacher but the facilitator of learning in my classroom, and my students drive the instruction each and every day. I am blessed to be an educator today and to see my students become leaders of technology!
(M. Lackey, personal communication, May 6, 2015)

LEARN FROM OUR PAST

To reach the same level of teaching achieved by Lackey, we must adjust our thinking and view technology in a different way than it was viewed two decades ago. When the technology door was first opened in the 1990s, we had no way of fully understanding how it would transform our world and be implemented in our schools. We knew technology could bring significant changes, but it was impossible to see its full potential. Technology is still evolving today, but we can see that technology and the Internet are not just resources that should occasionally be brought into classrooms and daily instruction—they should be the foundation of 21st century learning.

Today, few schools have the technology implemented in Clark Hall and other innovative learning spaces around the world that allows teachers and students to have access to devices, consistently log on, and have an almost infinite ability to surf, research, and create. Educators, like other professionals in the world, have had to learn some harsh lessons about hardware and networks. As we move forward, let's remember our mistakes and ideally not repeat them.

Most importantly, we must think differently when it comes to technology. We must adjust our priorities. Although some might say it can't be done, we must ask, "Why not?" and "If not now, then when?"

ENVISION HOW TECHNOLOGY AND SPACE CAN ENHANCE LEARNING

In the past, technology was implemented in schools without a clear vision for how to use it. Sometimes computers were placed in classrooms without plans for their usage, and entire labs were installed without clear guidelines for what could be accomplished.

As we make plans to tie technology into new types of learning space, it would be beneficial to have a clear vision of exactly where we wish to be with regard to current and future technology usage. Though it's hard to say with certainty exactly how technology will look beyond the next decade, we know in the next 10 years that online learning will expand from specific K–12 programs to stand-alone online courses at the high school level (and in some middle schools). Schools can start to discuss the role of blended learning and technology-based interventions and the general role technology will play in the curriculum, instruction, and assessment in the next decade. When teachers share the vision, they will also see the need for the training—and for a new type of space.

A key question in every school is whether to purchase laptops or tablets. There might not be a clear answer, but several factors should be considered to help form one. What age group will be using the devices and for what purposes? Can the tablets be readily adapted to use keyboards? Will the students be consumers or producers of information? Younger students who use graphics and touch screens to work through programs might be better served with tablets, but older students who are writing extensive papers and doing a great deal of research might need powerful laptops. It might be helpful to contact recent graduates and find out what they are using in college; this can provide some guidance for purchasing devices for the upper levels. We must create a technology plan that details if the district is going to use computer labs, have computers in each classroom, or push for one to one (1:1) computing in which all students have access to computers or other devices on a 24/7 basis.

Schools could begin by conducting internal audits to ascertain the current state of their technology. Questions that can be asked include, How many computers currently work? How many will we need to implement in our vision? Do we have the appropriate number of well-trained personnel devoted to maintaining our network? What kind of space will we need for the technology we wish to have?

As we design spaces for students to use technology, let's envision how they will use it there. A number of students will need to have their devices charging at the same time, which means new spaces might need additional electrical outlets. Furniture should be placed near the outlets so that cords may reach them. Also, envision the types of space that will fit multiple technology needs. Students can use technology to work independently or in small groups. The space and furniture should fit this vision. Large rooms will need projectors for students to make presentations. The curriculum, learning styles, and technology must all flow seamlessly together and be fulfilled through the learning space. In summary, technology will allow student groups to disperse and to learn at different paces in different ways; it will allow us to use space in ways that were not imaginable 20 years ago.

MODEL WITH OUR TEACHERS WHAT
WE EXPECT TO SEE IN OUR CLASSROOMS

For almost any initiative to be successful in a school, and especially one as complicated as technology usage, teachers must receive ongoing and embedded professional development; we must train teachers in how to use technology and how to let students use it. For too long, technology usage has been an occasional professional development topic or one that some teachers sought out on their own to enhance their own learning. Ironically, in the past two decades the bulk of professional development in America has been dedicated to implementing standards and preparing for state tests—as the Internet continued to grow and knowledge continued to double. We've been focusing on 20th century assessment models as the world raced away from us. If we are to use technology effectively in our 21st century learning space, we must elevate the importance of professional development dedicated to technology usage.

Just as importantly, the combination of the global economy, Generation Z, and 21st century technology has led to a fundamentally new way for students to use technology. It is no longer an extension of the teacher's lesson plan but more of a unique way for students to show what has been learned, and that's what needs to drive our professional development. In the days of computer labs, professional development began with how to use computers as word processors, and then it progressed to training teachers on what software could do to extend lessons, such as software for math or English classes. Today, a significant amount of professional development is provided to prepare teachers to use software that acts as an intervention to help students raise their standardized test scores. Students advance through levels of difficulty at different speeds as the program charts their progress and provides feedback to teachers. It is an amazing feat and shows the energy and money being devoted to test preparation.

But technology can do so much more today if teachers have the vision, funding, and training to push students to use it in exploring the 4 C's. For example, whereas teachers still need help in using some software programs designed to extend curriculum, they need more guidance on which websites can be effective resources for their students and how to help students create products and assess them. In professional development today, a balance must be struck between practices that promote traditional learning models and those that set students free to chart their own course in the new types of learning space. The same can be said of our teachers: will they be held in check by the system or allowed to improvise to find new methods?

Ideally, as teachers are trained they, too, are allowed to explore their learning in different spaces. Let them work alone in classrooms or in hallways or nooks that are designated study areas. Maybe they can have access to small conference rooms. Let them present to their peers on what they have learned and their implementation plans. When teachers experience it, they are more likely to use it. If we don't model it, then it's less likely to be used in classrooms.

OUR NETWORK MUST BE SO STRONG AND WELL MAINTAINED THAT IT RARELY CRASHES

We often have a sort of unspoken idea about school technology systems—that they will naturally be weaker than the ones used in the business sector, that somehow our students don't need the enterprise strength systems used by adults. Districts have often implemented systems with the minimal capacity, and the networks have often been too weak to support the computers as more devices came online. The systems limp along and quickly become obsolete. In many cases, students can't log on to the network, and instructional time is lost. Teachers become frustrated and often cease their attempts to transform their lessons.

Let's not view our technology systems as simple school technology systems; let's view them as complex systems that support hundreds or even thousands of individuals in an era of increasingly powerful apps and streaming options. It used to be only a few students at a time needed to be connected; now they all need to be online, especially in new learning spaces. In many cities, the schools will be the largest organization within the city boundaries to use technology. Let's not think of our schools as second-rate customers; let's view them as some of the city's largest businesses, the ones training our future leaders, workers, and artists. Let's view them as businesses in need of top-of-the-line technology. The future of our society hinges on the quality of its schools.

The technology team that maintains the system must be elevated in its importance. Technology directors must be both visionary and practical. One of the most important individuals in the entire district is the network engineer—the person who will have the greatest impact on the network's design and just as critically its problem solving. In many schools, teachers hold the dual roles of teacher and technology coordinator, and they often have difficulty finding time to fulfill both roles. We need a team of highly qualified technicians who are ready to react quickly as hardware, software, or network issues arise. This team can play a vital role in brainstorming with teachers in the activities students can complete in new types of learning space. They can work with teachers to let them know the capabilities of the systems, and they can adjust the hardware to help meet the needs of students and staff.

Computers in our schools are often not well maintained. Computers in every business need to be serviced; this is especially true in schools when the users are all young people. The team of technicians formed to maintain the technology has often been too small to meet the needs of the school. Today, many schools still don't understand that the quality and size of the technology team are two of the most important factors in the success of the district. Schools must have highly trained personnel who are available to solve technology problems as they arise. There must be minimal downtime for a malfunctioning computer; the computer must be repaired or traded for another one because student learning in the new space depends on it.

OUR TECHNOLOGY BUDGET MUST BE ROBUST

Districts have traditionally struggled to find the funds to upgrade the network or to replace computers. As district budgets shrank in the recession that began in 2008, technology funding was often among the first cuts. As the economy has rebounded, many districts still have not found the money to fund a costly expansion of technology. This will be an ongoing problem if school leaders continue to operate in a traditional mindset. Again, different times call for different ways of thinking. Schools must be bold.

In most schools, every dollar is already budgeted, so if we increase funding in one area it is often because of new revenue or a reallocation of funds. New funding often comes in the form of grants. Grants can be useful, but they are hard to acquire and require a great deal of follow-up procedures that require diligence and the use of personnel. They also can be restrictive in how the money is spent, which sometimes negates a school's ability to be creative as problems occur in the implementation process. However, if grants are the only viable option for upgrading technology and for funding professional development, then they should be pursued.

If a school reallocates funds from another area into technology, it means some painful choices must be made in the front end of the process as the money is taken from other key areas. However, once the decision is made and the money is allocated, the district is free to make adjustments throughout the implementation process, and unlike grants, there is no cumbersome follow-up reporting to the grant provider. Some school leaders will find the idea of reallocating existing funds to be politically impossible because of the anguish it will cause in the areas where the money is being withdrawn. Each school has its own culture and history that must be considered. One key to success in this technology shift is to provide constant communication to all parties about the need to elevate technology to the top of 21st century priorities; when people share the vision, they are more likely to understand and be cooperative. A new type of learning space calls for a new type of thinking. This will be a time for strong leadership. It's impossible for leaders to please everyone, but they must make key decisions that are in the long-term interests of students—and technology is one of these key areas.

Schools must also do all they can to drive down the costs of computer purchases and infrastructure upgrades. Almost every school has a partnership with a computer company from which it has purchased devices in previous years. The representatives of these companies should be brought into the dialogue early in the process so that they can hear the ideas and help form the vision. In many cases, the representatives will make more persuasive arguments with their superiors in the company when they can share the district vision, which could result in better deals for the districts. In addition, these companies usually have education specialists who can provide assistance, often at no charge to the schools.

Another key resource can be the parents of our students who are IT specialists. They can provide valuable advice if there are no other experts available. Care must be taken if these individuals are brought into the planning process to ensure they understand the district goals, politics, and funding realities.

Schools can also explore different purchasing options for funding and implementation. For example, as the cost for devices continues to drop they are becoming much more affordable for parents and students. Presently, many young people buy laptop computers immediately after they graduate from high school so that they will have a reliable device to use in college. At the high school level, educators can work with parents to shift their thinking to purchasing these computers during the high school years so they can use them to prepare for college work. If the computer is maintained properly, it can also serve as a college-level computer. Schools should explore purchasing options that help families through lease-to-own programs.

TEACH STUDENTS TO USE THE INTERNET ETHICALLY

As we promote new ways of teaching and the use of the Internet to foster creativity, we should also revisit our guidelines for use of the Internet and social media. It's just as important to be proactive with the staff as it will be with students; the staff should be trained on what is appropriate to post on a social media site, and discussions should be held on the age-level appropriateness of content with regard to violence, sex, and other contentious areas.

We must train our students on the ethical use of information, the importance of citing sources, and the consequences of plagiarism in the academic world. As with other serious transgressions, we must be firm and kind and have guidelines in place when these incidents occur.

Older students in a new learning space might spend more time working in groups or independently; thus, they might spend more time out of sight of the teacher and must be trusted to act responsibly. This takes training and dialogue with students to get them to understand they are being trusted to do the right thing, even when the teacher is not standing next to them. We must stress to students that they exercise self-discipline and remain on task.

Trust must go both ways; our students must trust that our teachers are providing relevant, interesting curriculum and fair and useful assessment models. If students are active partners in the learning process, they will have more buy-in to the entire learning process and are more likely to remain on task and act appropriately.

DISCUSS THE ROLE OF TECHNOLOGY IN TEACHER ASSESSMENT

As we move deeper into the challenges of shifting to 21st century education models, one question is the role of teacher assessment in implementing technology usage (and implementing global skills and adapting to Generation Z). For example, there are some members of our profession, as there are in all professions, who refuse to try new ideas and consequently keep their students locked in a substandard learning system. Where is the line between motivating teachers and forcing them to change? The greatest results are often achieved by motivated professional educators when they see a need for improvement, receive adequate training and support, and work together to devise ways of achieving their goals. As we move into a new type of learning space, how do we create a teacher assessment system that can motivate and educate professionals yet still be strong enough to deal with those who do not wish to grow? And when the adaptations involving global skills, Generation Z, and technology are actually implemented, how can they be assessed? It comes back to one of the basic questions of teaching: how do we accurately assess student learning?

REALIZE THIS IS A CAREER-LONG INITIATIVE

Educators often view improvement initiatives through 9-month lenses. However, the rest of the world doesn't function in that time frame, and if we are to make this transition into a new way of teaching we must view it as an ongoing process that will take more than 9 months. Whereas some people and schools could move quickly into a new model, others will take more than 9 months, perhaps even years. We must view our technology evolution as one that will occur for the rest of our careers, not just during this one school year. This concept also applies to learning space; the learning space of tomorrow could be different based on the technology used, the skills needed, and the learning styles of the students.

TURN TO THE TRUE EXPERTS: OUR STUDENTS

To shift our thinking to digital teaching and learning we don't have to be technology experts, but a shift of this magnitude calls for new lifelines of support. More than ever, we must ask for help from our peers. And luckily, we are surrounded by *hundreds* of digital experts—our students. When in doubt on what to do, we can ask them. We can pull a student aside for a private chat or ask a class, "Is there a better way of doing this assignment by using your computers, tablets, or cell phones? Is there a better way of using this space?" We don't have to make this shift alone.

The biggest obstacle we have is not technological or pedagogical. It's mental. An overarching question for educators is whether we have the courage to turn our students loose to learn in ways in which we don't control every part of the process. When we expose more of the world to our students, they might not always agree with what we say, or they might begin to view the world differently from the way we do. The answers they give us and the work they submit might be different from what we have seen in the past because we are no longer guiding every step of their learning.

To make this shift to a new learning space and to use technology appropriately, we must overcome our fears of losing control and of not having all of the answers. Teachers have been trained to always have the class under the tightest curricular, teaching, and assessment bonds, and we can always report what has been taught in the past, what is presently occurring, and where the teaching and learning are going. However, when we give more freedom to our students to plug into technology and to sometimes move out of sight as they work, we must be brave enough and possess the flexibility and confidence to constantly adjust. We can have set standards, objectives, and benchmarks, but the best learning is often unscripted. We must find the balance between guiding our students and controlling the outcomes. This is the true art of teaching.

PROFESSIONAL DEVELOPMENT
ACTIVITIES TO HELP STUDENTS USE TECHNOLOGY
Collaboration

- Examine your Internet polices with fellow educators and determine if they are adequate for today's teachers and students.

- Discuss the challenges of citing online sources and avoiding academic dishonesty with students.

- Work with your peers and students to determine the advantages and disadvantages of tablets and laptop computers.

- Ask students how they would use technology in schools if they were given the freedom.

- Discuss the potential of finding funds for technology upgrades, including the possibility of obtaining grants or of shifting funds within the current budget.

- Determine if there are any parents or technology experts in the community who might volunteer their services to help the school.

Creativity

- Create guidelines for social media usage for both students and staff.

- Form a realistic technology plan that incorporates upgrades in the infrastructure and a schedule for more computer or tablet implementation.

Critical Thinking

- Discuss with colleagues and students the impact on teaching if students are empowered to take more control of their learning through the use of technology.

- Imagine a fair and efficient teacher assessment model that incorporates student use of technology into its domains.

- Examine your school's discipline records to determine the types of Internet-related offenses created in the past 2 years and begin to think of initiatives and policies to help students deal with these types of offenses.

Communicating

- Educate people on the importance of having a strong network. Begin to shift their thinking to understanding that technology will be the foundation of 21st century teaching.

- Let students, parents, and the community know about the import-ant conversations you are having concerning laptops and tablets, ways to use technology in classrooms and to improve a school's efficiency, and the school's plan for moving forward.

- Share success stories with students, staff, and the community.

Stretch to the Future

- Imagine the changes in the school when we only need half of our current high school space because half of the students are taking blended or online courses.

- Begin to imagine how to use the additional space in your school when fewer classrooms are needed.

- Brainstorm about what technology will be in classrooms up to 30 years from now.

Blended and Online Learning

Examine the status of blended and online courses in your school. Ask if they are working and what needs to be done to improve them and then decide if there are courses that can be moved online or blended in the future.

NAME OF COURSE	IS IT ONLINE OR BLENDED?	IS IT WORKING?	WHAT NEEDS TO BE DONE TO IMPROVE IT?

What course could be blended or moved online in the future?

NAME OF COURSE	WILL IT BE ONLINE OR BLENDED?	WHO WILL TEACH IT?	WHAT IS THE TIME LINE FOR IMPLEMENTATION?	WHAT IS NEEDED TO MAKE IT SUCCESSFUL?

Professional Development

Create a professional development plan in which teachers design learning space around technology usage.

UNIT, LESSON, OR ACTIVITY IN YOUR CURRICULUM	ARE STUDENTS COLLABORATING?	ARE STUDENTS THINKING CRITICALLY?	ARE STUDENTS CREATING?	ARE STUDENTS COMMUNICATING?	WHAT KIND OF SPACE DO YOU NEED, AND HOW WILL IT BE USED?

Technology Resources

Identify sources of information that can be used for your own research or shared with others. Examples of resources include students, books and periodicals, staff members, other schools or districts, educational consultants, IT professionals, websites, blogs, education conferences, and others sources that you deem appropriate.

TYPE OF RESOURCE	WHAT DOES THE RESOURCE PROVIDE?	WHO ARE THE MAIN INDIVIDUALS TO CONTACT IN THIS RESOURCE?	WHAT ARE OTHER IMPORTANT FACTORS ABOUT THIS RESOURCE?
Students			
Books and periodicals			
Staff members			
Other schools or districts			
Educational consultants			
IT professionals			
Websites			
Blogs			
Education conferences			

Works Cited

"21st Century Fluencies | Global Digital Citizen Foundation." Global Digital Citizen Foundation. N.p., n.d. Web. 15 May 2015.

"About the Standards." Common Core State Standards Initiative. About the Standards Comments. N.p., n.d. Web. 15 May 2015.

Akin, Monta. E-mail interview. 29 April 2015.

Clamp, Luke. E-mail interview. 30 June 2015.

"Dell Executive Briefing." Personal interview. Feb. 2010.

Dodd, Bobby. E-mail interview. 1 June 2015.

Domine, April. E-mail interview. 9 August 2015.

"EnGauge 21st Century Skills." Metiri Group | Meteri Group, n.d. Web. 15 May 2015.

Friedman, Thomas L. "Need a Job? Invent It." *New York Times*. 30 Mar. 2013. Web. 15 May 2015.

Gleek, Ann. E-mail interview. 26 February 2015.

Gregory, Karie. E-mail interview. 12 May 2015.

Jasper, Debra. E-mail interview. 24 May 2015.

Klein, Erin. E-mail interview. 3 May 2015.

Lackey, Martha. E-mail interview. 6 May 2015.

"Lao Tzu." *BBC News*. BBC. n.d. Web. 5 July 2015.

Madhavan, Santosh. E-mail interview. 1 May 2015.

Marshall, Dwayne. E-mail interview. 27 April 2015.

"The Professional Learning Community for 21st Century Education Leaders." *EdLeader21*. N.p., n.d., Web. 15 May 2015.

Rothman, Darla. "A Tsunami of Learners Called Generation Z." *MDLE*, n.p., n. d. Web.

Rivera, Alejandra. E-mail interview. 11 April 2015.

Schilling, David Russell. "Knowledge Doubling Every 12 Months, Soon to Be Every 12 Hours." Web log post citing IBM. Industry Tap Into News. Industry Tap, 19 April 2013. Web. 16 May 2015.

"Skills," n.d. Web. 15 May 2015. P21 Common Core Toolkit—P21. Partnership for 21st Century.

Sturchio, Emily. E-mail interview. 1 May 2015.

"Understanding the Skills in the Common Core State Standards." *Achieve*, Dec. 2012. Web. 15 May 2015.

Wise, Brent. E-mail interview. 14 April 2015.

Index

A SAGE Publishing Company

Helping educators make the greatest impact

CORWIN HAS ONE MISSION: to enhance education through intentional professional learning.

We build long-term relationships with our authors, educators, clients, and associations who partner with us to develop and continuously improve the best evidence-based practices that establish and support lifelong learning.

Solutions you want. Experts you trust. Results you need.

Author Consulting

AUTHOR CONSULTING

On-site professional learning with sustainable results! Let us help you design a professional learning plan to meet the unique needs of your school or district. www.corwin.com/pd

Institutes

INSTITUTES

Corwin Institutes provide collaborative learning experiences that equip your team with tools and action plans ready for immediate implementation. www.corwin.com/institutes

eCourses

ECOURSES

Practical, flexible online professional learning designed to let you go at your own pace. www.corwin.com/ecourses

Read2Earn

READ2EARN

Did you know you can earn graduate credit for reading this book? Find out how: www.corwin.com/read2earn

Contact an account manager at (800) 831-6640 or visit www.corwin.com for more information.